THE KLAUSENBERGER
REBBE
Rebuilding

THE KLAUSENBERGER
REBBE

Rebuilding

Translated and adapted by
Judah Lifschitz
from *Lapid HaEish* by Aharon Surasky

A TARGUM PRESS Book

First published 2007
Copyright © 2007 by Judah Lifschitz
ISBN 978-1-56871-451-6

Translated and adapted with the permission of Yechezkel Shraga Frankel from the Hebrew work *Lapid HaEish*.

Published by:
TARGUM PRESS, INC.
22700 W. Eleven Mile Rd.
Southfield, MI 48034
E-mail: targum@netvision.net.il
Fax: 888-298-9992
www.targum.com

Distributed by:
FELDHEIM PUBLISHERS
202 Airport Executive Park
Nanuet, NY 10954

Printing plates by Frank, Jerusalem
Printed in Israel by Chish Press

Photo credits: Yechezkel Shraga Frankel

Rabbi CHAIM P. SCHEINBERG
Rosh Hayeshiva "TORAH ORE"
and Morah Hora'ah of Kiryat Mattersdorf

הרב חיים פינחס שיינברג
ראש ישיבת "תורה אור"
ומורה הוראה דקרית מטרסדורף

ערב ראש השנה תשס"ח

<u>מכתב ברכה</u>

It was my pleasure to receive a draft of Mr. Judah Lifschitz's forthcoming book, a translation of Lapid HaEish. The receipt of the draft was especially meaningful because of the very close bond the author had as a student of my dear brother, Harav Shmuel Scheinberg zt"l. Mr. Lifschitz stands out amongst my brother's former students because of his sincere love for Torah values, his personal and business integrity and his enthusiasm for sharing his Torah and professional knowledge with others. This masterful translation of Lapid HaEish will surely bring his readers to ever greater heights of יראת שמים and a desire to improve in their בין אדם למקום and בין אדם לחברו.

הכו"ח בברכת כתיבה וחתימה טובה

רחוב פנים מאירות 2, ירושלים, ת.ד. 6979, טל. 537-1513 (02), ישראל
2 Panim Meirot St., Jerusalem, P.O.B 8979, Tel (02) 537-1513, Israel

THE YESHIVA
OF GREATER WASHINGTON

ב"ה

It is with great pleasure that I take pen in hand to warmly endorse the latest work of our wonderful community *askan*, Mr. Judah Lifschitz. Mr. Lifschitz has taken upon himself the important task of bringing to the English-speaking public a great work - Rabbi Aharon Sorsky's classic "Lapid HaEish", the biography of the Klausenberger Rebbe, Rabbi Yekusiel Yehudah Halberstam *zy"a*. We do not, today, truly comprehend the difficulties of life during the Holocaust, and the rebuilding years that followed. It is only by reading and reflecting upon the actions of Gedolei Yisroel and their followers during the terrible Churban that we can achieve some measure of understanding. Mr. Lifschitz's efforts to effectuate the translation of the Hebrew edition speak volumes as to his own understanding and drive to be *mezakeh* the *rabbim* and to be *mechanech* the next *dor* of *bnei* and *bnos Torah*.

Bebircas HaTorah,

Rabbi Gedaliah Anemer

In honor of my beloved
marah d'asrah, rosh hayeshivah, and rebbe

Rabbi Gedaliah Anemer, שליט״א
and
Rebbetzin Yocheved Anemer, ת׳ לרפו״ש

May HaKadosh Baruch Hu bless you with
arichas yamim veshanim in good health
and happiness.

In loving memory
of my beloved father

Morris Lifschitz, ז״ל
משה בן נחום

who taught me, by example, that life is meaningful
only when it is dedicated to the service of Hashem
and the love of family.

נלב״ע ערב סוכות תשמ״ו

ת.נ.צ.ב.ה.

Dedicated in memory
of a legendary Klausenberger chassid
Rabbi Yehudah Turner, זצ״ל

לעילוי ולטובת נשמת אבי מורי היקר באדם
מוהרר״ר **יהודה** ב״ר **שבתי** זצ״ל
נלב״ע ז׳ שבט תש״מ
ת.נ.צ.ב.ה.

שהיה אדוק בכל לבו ונפשו בדביקות אמת ברבו כ״ק מרן אדמו״ר זי״ע
והיה מראשוני העסקנים שלא ע״מ לקבל פרס לעמוד לימין צדקו
בכל מפעלותיו הקדושים ובפרט בבנין בית החולים.

In loving memory of my beloved mother
Rebbetzin Chaya Chana Turner, ע״ה

ולעילוי נשמת אמי מורתי
מרת **חנה חיה** בת **ברוך** ע״ה
נלב״ע כ״ד ניסן תשס״ה
ת.נ.צ.ב.ה.

שעמדה לימין בעלה בכל פעולתיו למען הכלל והפרט
וביתה היתה פתוחה לרווחה לכל נצרך.

הרשל טורנר ומשפחתו

In loving memory of our beloved father,
father-in-law, and grandfather,

Reb Yitzchak Glassman, ע״ה

whose complete faith, unconditional love,
honesty, humility, and good-hearted nature
are an everlasting legacy.

לעילוי נשמת חמי הר״ר **יצחק** ב״ר **משה** ז״ל

נלב״ע י״ב ניסן תשס״ה

ת.נ.צ.ב.ה.

הרשל טורנר ומשפחתו

Contents

Translator's Preface

It was at the casual suggestion of my dear friend Rabbi Aaron Lopiansky, *shlita,* that I read the first volume of *Lapid HaEish*, the inspirational biography of the Klausenberger Rebbe, Rabbi Yekusiel Yehudah Halberstam, *zy"a,* written by Aharon Surasky and published by Yechezkel Shraga Frankel, *z"l.* The truth be told, at that time, I was not at all acquainted with the Klausenberger Rebbe. The Rebbe had passed away several years before and I had no previous connection to him, to his writings, or to Sanz-Klausenberg Chassidus. In fact, I took up the suggestion that I read the book simply because of my general interest in biographies of *gedolim*. Little did I know that this particular biography would have a lasting effect on my life and my personal approach to *Yiddishkeit*.

How could the Klausenberger Rebbe, with whom I had no personal relationship or contact, become, years after his death, such an important influence in my life? Perhaps the answer can be found in the Rebbe's own teachings. In a Chumash and *Rashi* shiur (*Parashas Ki Sisa,* 5742) the Rebbe identified

certain eternal characteristics of a tzaddik. Even after his departure from this world, the tzaddik prays for the welfare of every
Jew, seeking mercy for each Jew and for *klal Yisrael* as a whole.
From his eternal resting place in the heavens above, the tzaddik,
through his study of Torah, is empowered to eradicate evil de-
crees against individual Jews and the Jewish people; for a
"tzaddik commands and HaKadosh Baruch Hu fulfills his command." Thus, even after death, tzaddikim remain our protec-
tors and benefactors, looking out for our welfare and assisting
us in reaching our spiritual potential. How important it is, then,
for every Jew to become and remain connected to the eternal influence of a tzaddik.

Soon after the publication of *The Klausenberger Rebbe: The
War Years*, I received letters and e-mails from Jews far and wide,
each with a personal vignette of how they had been affected by
the life story of the Klausenberger Rebbe. For some it was a
source of *chizuk* in difficult times. For others it was a lesson in
faith and *bitachon*. For yet others it was encouragement to strive
for greater achievements in Torah and mitzvos. For all, however,
the Rebbe had become a fountain of inspiration. These personal
reflections, together with my own experience, motivated me,
with the Almighty's assistance, to translate and adapt volume
two of *Lapid HaEish*.

It is with an abundance of gratitude to HaKadosh Baruch
Hu that I have completed the second volume of the biography of
the Rebbe, which focuses on the Rebbe's extraordinary efforts
to rebuild, out of the ashes of the Holocaust, the glorious
Sanz-Klausenberg chassidic dynasty. In this volume we follow
the Rebbe from his immigration to the United States in 1947 to

his rebuilding of Sanz-Klausenberg Chassidus, its communities and Torah and chesed institutions in New York and then to his aliyah to Israel and his building of Kiryat Sanz in Netanyah. The Klausenberger's postwar accomplishments were enormous under any standard, but even more so when viewed against the backdrop of his personal tragedies and the destruction of European Jewry during the Holocaust. It is my hope and prayer that the story of the Rebbe's rebuilding will be as meaningful as those of the war years.

Once again I have been blessed by Hashem to reach this day only through His benevolence and the assistance and encouragement of others. Briefly, I wish to express my *hakaras hatov* to those who have assisted me.

First and foremost, my wife Marilyn, our children Pirchie and Yosef, Nachum and Jen, Tamar and Dovid, and our grandchildren Moshe, Adina, Yakov, and Hillel, *ken yirbu*, are a constant and my most important source of support and motivation. May each of them carry deep into their hearts the lessons of the Klausenberger Rebbe's life, and may they strive each and every day to achieve greater heights in *avodas Hashem*.

My father *z"l*, my mother *tb"l*, and my in-laws have been life-long role models. May Hashem grant them good health, joy, and *nachas, ad me'ah ve'esrim shanah*. My brother, sisters-in-law, and brothers-in-law, and their families are important parts of my life and I am forever thankful for their love.

This book, like *The Klausenberger Rebbe: The War Years*, is the product of a partnership, *lesheim shamayim*, with Rabbi Heshy Turner. It is Rabbi Turner who first enabled me to translate the Rebbe's biography and it is he who has continued to provide encouragement and support. More than my partner, Rabbi Turner has become a beloved *chaver* and role model.

I am blessed with very special partners Ron Shapiro and Steve Schram who, in addition to being outstanding attorneys, are men of great compassion and generosity.

For thirty years I have been blessed to live in Silver Spring, Maryland, a community where, due to the dedication of the community's *rabbanim* and leaders, growth in Torah, mitzvos, and *middos* is not simply a goal but a way of life. I especially cherish my hours in the *beis midrash* of the Yeshiva of Greater Washington. Each of the individuals with whom I am fortunate to learn has a very special place in my life and to each, my *daf yomi chaverim* and Rabbi Eli Reingold, I am eternally grateful. A very special thank you to my *yedid nefesh*, Rabbi Zev Katz, *menahel* of the Girl's School of the Yeshiva, for his constant support, advice, and genuine friendship.

When I first started to write I was introduced to Rabbi Moshe Dombey, *z"l*, and Targum Press. Rabbi Dombey, in his quiet, unassuming, but highly talented way, transformed my concepts and manuscripts into published books. His untimely *petirah* was a terrible loss for all who knew him. May his memory be for a blessing.

I am very appreciative of the wonderful and talented professionals at Targum Press, who time and again provide me with expert advice and insight. My editor Chaya Baila Gavant deserves a very special recognition for her dedication to this project.

As I complete this book, I fervently pray that Hashem bless

this endeavor and enable these humble pages to bring inspiration and *chizuk* to those who read them. In the merit of the holy Klausenberger Rebbe, *zy"a,* may we be blessed with peace, tranquility, and the coming of Mashiach, soon and in our days, Amen.

Judah Lifschitz
Elul 5767

Introduction

If a man resolves firmly not to be swayed from his faith, not even an iota, and declares that even if he were placed between two millstones or his flesh stripped with iron combs like Rabbi Akiva in his time, that he will not sin and will declare that the Almighty is the One and only G-d, then his end will be like Iyov who, after all his suffering – his property destroyed, his wife and children dead – it was said of him, "You still retain your faith" (Iyov 2:9). Because Iyov did not complain, at the very end, "the Almighty blessed the latter end of Iyov more than his beginning and he was never tested again" (Ibid. 42:12).

How great is the power of faith! Chazal have taught us, "The end of the exiles will occur only as a reward for faith in the Almighty." That is the cause of all the great and terrible challenges confronting today's generation. Beginning with Hitler, may his name be erased forever, even before and through the present, the verse in Tehillim, "Behold, these are the wicked, always at ease; they increase in riches," has been fulfilled, while those who fear the word of G-d live a life of suffering and difficulty.

Thus, it is incumbent on each one of us to strengthen and deepen our belief in the Almighty; that He is righteous; that we are unable to understand His ways. We must give thanks and praise to the Master of the Universe that He did not create us like the nations of the world and did not cast our lot among those who do not believe in Him. We become stronger through a simple faith that the Almighty is the Lord. "He gives us strength to make wealth." "He provides sustenance to all, from the tiny eggs of lice to the rams of the bison," and it is in Him that we place our hopes. In the merit of this faith we will witness the fulfillment of the verse, "The Lord is on my side; I will not fear; what can man do to me? For only if one's faith weakens can he be harmed."

(*Shefa Chaim, Derashos Chumash V'Rashi* 5742,
Parashas Behar-Bechukosai)

The Rebbe's Early Years

Appreciation of the magnitude of the Klausenberger Rebbe's postwar rebuilding efforts and accomplishments can only be gained after first contemplating the enormity of the Rebbe's suffering and the challenges he faced and overcame during the dark days of Hitler's reign.

The Klausenberger Rebbe, Rabbi Yekusiel Yehudah Halberstam, was a young man of thirty-five when World War II broke out in 1939. A descendant of important chassidic families, the Rebbe was a great-grandson of Rabbi Chaim of Sanz, the Divrei Chaim. His father, Rabbi Tzvi Hirsch, was the *rav* of Rudnick, Galicia, and his mother was a descendant of both the B'nei Yissaschar, Rabbi Elimelech Shapiro of Dinov, and the

Ateres Tzvi, Rabbi Tzvi Hirsch Eichenstein of Ziditchov. The Klausenberger was born on 4 Shevat 1905 (5665) in Rudnick, where his father served as *rav*.

From Yekusiel Yehudah's earliest years, his father, who was his primary teacher, instilled in him a love of Torah and fear of Heaven. During World War I, the family was forced to flee Rudnick and settled in Kleinvardein, where they remained for six years. Rabbi Tzvi Hirsch passed away during this time, when Yekusiel Yehudah was a mere thirteen.

Despite being orphaned at such a young age, the young Yekusiel Yehudah learned a great deal from his saintly father: the fundamentals of Torah learning, Kabbalah, and the chassidic way of life, and, most important of all, his extraordinary character traits. The spirituality which he observed from his father became Yekusiel Yehudah's way of life. Years later the Klausenberger would say of his father's influence, "Everything I heard and saw of my father remained etched in my memory forever. Even the things I witnessed when I was very young I remember well. I shall never forget a thing...not even a simple gesture of his."

Reb Tzvi Hirsch instilled in his son a love for the teachings of the Divrei Chaim. "All his life my father would talk about Sanz. Just as a person does not forget that he is alive, so my father did not stop thinking, even for a moment, about my holy great-grandfather the Divrei Chaim. But we did not hear stories of miracles. Rather, he would only tell us about the Divrei Chaim's way of serving Hashem — how he davened and learned Torah, how he recited Hallel, how he conducted his holy *tisch*, what he would do before davening and what he would do after —

things from which we could learn to serve Hashem."

After his father's death, Yekusiel Yehudah put all his efforts into learning Torah. He soon became known as the *ilui* of Rudnick. He studied with several great chassidic rebbes, including the Imrei Emes, Rabbi Meir Yechiel of Ostrovtza, Rabbi Chaim Eliezer Shapiro of Munkatch (author of the *Minchas Eliezer*), and others. He was acquainted with many of the greatest chassidic rebbes of the time.

Marriage and Relocation to Klausenberg

In 1925, at the age of twenty, the young Yekusiel Yehudah married Pessel Teitelbaum, daughter of Rav Chaim Tzvi, the *rav* of Sighet, known as the Atzei Chaim, a descendant of the Divrei Chaim. Eleven children were born to them before World War II intervened.

For the first two years of his marriage, the Klausenberger remained in Sighet learning Torah from his father-in-law, who loved him dearly. Then, in 1927, he assumed the position of *rav* of Klausenberg, the capital of Transylvania (now Romania).

The Jewish community of Klausenberg had a long history, dating back to 1591. In 1927 it boasted a population of sixteen thousand Jews, the majority of whom were irreligious and associated with either communist or Zionist groups. The Orthodox community was in a weakened state. Recognizing the gravity of the situation, a group of chassidic Jews formed their own minyan and hired the Klausenberger as their new *rav*.

Although he was perhaps the youngest *rav* in the country, Rav Yekusiel Yehudah immediately made an impact on his new community. His charismatic personality attracted even the more modern and less-observant segments of the Jewish community. His love for all Jews, including the nonreligious, was enormous.

For himself the Klausenberger was content to make do with the bare minimum. Often he gave his own meal to a hungry yeshivah student or guest, although he was careful that his *rebbetzin* would not see what he was doing. When he saw that an impoverished man in the community, ill and starving, was left unattended due to his sickly appearance and unpleasant body odor, the Klausenberger personally took him into his home, fed him, and cared for him until he returned to health. (Later in life, the Rebbe would credit this act of kindness with saving him from the crematoria.)

The Rebbe waged a continuous battle against his material and physical needs. His daily schedule was not that of a typical man. He immersed himself in the *mikveh* many times, denied himself the enjoyment of food and drink, ate bread only on Shabbos and *yamim tovim*, and often ate but a single meal a day. He slept a mere three hours a night, generally on a bench in the *beis midrash*, spending the rest of the night learning Torah. His prayers to the Almighty, punctuated by cries and groans, were ablaze with the fire of his spirit. He would stand before his Creator totally immersed in his love for Him.

The hallmark of the Rebbe's years in Klausenberg was his efforts in teaching Torah. Soon after he arrived, he established a yeshivah where he taught several hours a day and in which many exceptional students studied.

Revered by the community, the Klausenberger soon became well known throughout the area. His years in Klausenberg were marked by the visits of many great rabbinic and chassidic leaders. From time to time he was offered rabbinic positions in other areas, including a position on the *beis din* of Rabbi Yosef Tzvi Dushinsky in Yerushalayim, but he always declined.

World War II

The outbreak of World War II opened before the Klausenberger an abyss of darkness and loss. Yet despite the terrible suffering and tragedies that he endured, the Rebbe clung to his faith in his Savior, the G-d of Yaakov. All of his strength came from the fact that Hashem was his G-d. He did not need anything more than that.

During the first few years of the war, when Polish and Lithuanian Jewry was being slaughtered en masse, the Jews of Romania and Hungry were still living a relatively "normal" existence. The tragedy that awaited them came only during the last year of the war. During these early years, however, the Jews of Hungary and Romania were persecuted daily. The fierce anti-Semitism and hatred grew to such extreme proportions that every Jew felt his life was imperiled.

In the summer of 1940, after the Vienna Accords were executed, Transylvania was divided into three countries, and the city of Klausenberg, which had been the capital of Transylvania, was thereafter ruled by the Magyars, who were Nazi collaborators. At the end of the summer of 1940 the Hungarian army entered the Klausenberg area and the Jews were overcome with fear.

The Rebbe, however, was steadfast in his faith in the Almighty and continued to serve his followers with great strength and devotion. The Hungarian soldiers and police constantly harassed the Jews in the area, and many of them were afraid to leave their houses. The Rebbe, however, remained unafraid. Even when passing a group of Hungarian soldiers armed with revolvers and obviously looking to cause trouble, he would remain calm, reciting words of *emunah* and *bitachon* until the danger was over and serving as a calming presence for his followers.

Because the Klausenberger Rebbe had been born in Galicia, he was officially considered a Polish citizen, which meant that his days in Hungary were numbered. One day a squad of Hungarian soldiers came to his house with an official government order to take the Rebbe and his family away to a central location in Budapest, where all the deportees were being assembled.

Once in Budapest, the Rebbe was separated from his family and imprisoned with other VIPs who were going to be transported by the Nazis across the border. The *rebbetzin* and the children were taken to a temporary prison camp for foreigners, near Budapest, until their fate was determined.

After a concerted effort by close friends and supporters of the Rebbe, the Agency for the Protection of Rights of Hungarian Jewry interceded with the authorities on the Rebbe's behalf. The Klausenberger was released from the group he had been a part of and transferred to the prison camp for deportees where his wife and children were imprisoned. After several weeks of determined efforts by leaders of the Klausenberg and Budapest Jewish communities, the Rebbe and his family were allowed to return home.

Although the situation in Klausenberg was going from bad

to worse, the Rebbe refused to leave his followers and made no effort to leave the city. Instead, he opened his home to the Jewish refugees who streamed into the city ahead of the advancing German army, even though this endangered his own life even further. Even during the mad days of terror from 1941 to 1944, the Rebbe never stopped learning and davening and pleading on behalf of the Jewish People. He completely forgot about himself and was concerned only with the plight of his brethren. Sensing what lay ahead, he devoted all his energies to alleviating the burdens of his tortured followers by elevating them to higher worlds.

On Sunday, 24 Adar 5704 (1944), the Nazis invaded Hungary, the last European country that still had a large concentration of Jews, and seized the country in a raging fury. The one million Hungarian Jews were now confronted with the sword of destruction dangling over their heads.

Time was beginning to work against the Nazis. The Soviet army had already begun its powerful counteroffensive, regaining control of the Ukraine as it advanced on the Carpathian Mountains. The bloodthirsty Nazis were worried, with good reason, about their impending defeat. Yet they relentlessly pursued their primary goal of the destruction of the Jewish people.

Under the command of Adolph Eichmann, the Nazis pounced on their prey with single-minded viciousness. Before long, transports of Jews were being sent to Auschwitz, where the newly constructed gas chambers enabled the murder of over ten thousand Jews a day.

It was well known that the Nazis always began their rule by capturing the spiritual leaders of a community. Thus, when the

SS entered Klausenberg and took charge of the city, the Rebbe slipped out of his house and hid for several weeks in a cemetery on the outskirts of the town. In Iyar 1944 the Klausenberger entered the city of Banya and was conscripted into a forced labor camp, along with some five thousand other Jews who had been transported there for labor by the Hungarian army.

In the Concentration Camps

From Banya the Rebbe was transported across the Polish border together with thousands of other Jews, to the death camp of Auschwitz. At around the same time, the Jews of Klausenberg were being sent in mass numbers to their deaths in the gas chambers. On June 2, 1944 (11 Sivan 5704), the Rebbetzin and the nine children who were with her at the time were murdered by the Nazis.

The Klausenberger mourned this loss deeply. After the war he would cry bitterly at *Parashas Vayishlach*, which relates the story of Yaakov Avinu's efforts to protect his household from his brother, Eisav. "Like Yaakov, I took my family and eleven children across a river; they crossed a river of blood along with multitudes of holy and pure Jews," the Rebbe would say.

Upon his arrival in Auschwitz, the Rebbe was selected for work by the infamous Nazi butcher, Dr. Joseph Mengele. Saved from the gas chamber, the Rebbe was sentenced to a life worse than death. It was here that the Klausenberger was elevated to great and lofty levels of service of Hashem, publicly sanctifying his Creator's name with every action.

The Rebbe's incredibly saintly behavior during his imprisonment in Auschwitz and other concentration camps was an amazing thing to behold, almost beyond the comprehension of an ordinary mortal. Although the Rebbe was physically a part of the world around him, mentally and spiritually he was on a completely different plane. The lives of the prisoners in Auschwitz were unlike the lives of people anywhere else in the world. Yet the Klausenberger Rebbe managed to create for himself an island of purity and holiness in the midst of the horrors.

Most of the inmates in the concentration camp could think of nothing but their own tortured existence. The Klausenberger, however, put his thoughts on spiritual matters, longing to put on tefillin, wash his hands in the morning, daven, and observe the *yamim tovim*. He ached for the Almighty, who was suffering along with His people — as the verse says, "For I am with you in times of trouble."

When things were particularly difficult and the prisoners lay hopelessly on the floor, bleeding from their many wounds, the Klausenberger could be heard murmuring, "From Your place, our King, You will appear and reign over us, for we await You!"

Even during the most terrible times, the Rebbe never lost his focus on *avodas Hashem*. Under the very noses of the Nazis, he studied Torah, davened, and observed the mitzvos. Without regard for his personal safety, he avoided even the most minor transgression of Torah law.

Labor Detail in Warsaw

After the failed Warsaw Ghetto uprising during Pesach of 1943, the Nazis liquidated the ghetto, destroying the remains of what had once been the largest Jewish community in Europe. A year later, some thirty thousand Hungarian Jews were brought to the city to collect the valuables left in the ghetto and salvage the bricks and steel that remained there so that it could be sold to Polish contractors. Among these Jews was the Klausenberger Rebbe.

The work of clearing the ruins was both difficult and dangerous. The Jewish prisoners were forced to dig under the foundations of the bombed-out buildings, tie ropes to the walls, and pull on the ropes until the walls crumbled and fell. Sometimes the falling walls collapsed on the laborers and buried them alive. Often as they cleared out the ruins, they would uncover bunkers full of corpses, the remains of Jews who had been shot or gassed or had succumbed to hunger and disease.

When it became clear to the Germans that they would not be able to withstand the oncoming Russian offensive, they decided to finish off the temporary camp in the Warsaw Ghetto, and the prisoners who had been working there for several months, the Klausenberger among them, were taken to a field outside of Warsaw for execution. Once in the field, the prisoners were ordered to strip their clothes and approach the ditches. However, just before the planned execution, a high-ranking SS officer drove up and announced that there had been a change of plans: the prisoners were needed at the Dachau concentration camp.

The Rebbe's life was spared once again in this miraculous event. The prisoners were ordered to get dressed again and were soon organized for the march to Dachau, which was located in Germany.

Working in the Muldorf Forest

After an arduous trek, during which thousands of prisoners perished, the prisoners arrived in Dachau, where the Klausenberger was assigned to a labor group that was to work in the Muldorf Forest.

The Rebbe spent the last eight months of the war in this area, a concentration and work camp approximately fifty miles from Munich. There he was put to work constructing a subterranean hangar as well as missile batteries which the Germans planned to use for bombing large European cities. The laborers in Muldorf spent twelve hours a day in backbreaking labor. In addition, the construction site was located at a distance of five miles from the bunkers, and the prisoners were forced to march there by foot every day. The return trip, after an entire day of hard labor, was almost beyond endurance.

Yet despite the torturous labor and work conditions, the Rebbe's burning love for his Creator remained as strong as ever. The Nazis ruled over his physical being with great cruelty, but they had no control over his spirit and soul. He was one of the freest men ensnared by the Nazi regime.

The many recollections of Muldorf survivors combine to provide a clear and detailed picture of the Rebbe during that very difficult time. Despite the satanic cruelty to which he was constantly subjected, the Rebbe was concerned only with serving Hashem and fulfilling the Torah and mitzvos. His obligations to the Almighty were the same whether he was sitting comfortably and peacefully as the leader of Klausenberg Jewry or whether he was a prisoner trampled beneath the feet of the Nazis.

Together with his fellow prisoners, the Rebbe celebrated the *yamim noraim* of 1944 in the Muldorf concentration camp, davening secretly for redemption. With a fiery spirit, the Klausenberger called upon each prisoner to strengthen his faith, since they were all children of the Almighty. Surely, the Rebbe assured his fellow inmates, in the same way that a father has mercy on his children, so G-d would have mercy on them. The redemption would come in the blink of an eye. "We must have faith in Hashem that we will outlive all our enemies," he declared.

Months later, when Pesach of 1945 approached, the Rebbe began making preparations for the holiday, paying no attention to the chains of his Nazi bondage. With his faith in the Almighty, he was completely unconcerned about how he would sustain himself during the eight days of the holiday, when he would not eat even the smallest crumb of *chametz*. He was certain that he would be able to recite the blessing over matzah on the first night of Pesach. Sure enough, matzos were baked in secret and a true seder was conducted in the Muldorf barracks, led by the Klausenberger Rebbe, the Visheva Rebbe, and several others.

Liberation

The day after Pesach, after having survived the entire holiday on almost no food, the Rebbe told a young inmate, "My heart tells me that our redemption is very near." Three weeks later, the American army reached Muldorf and liberated the prisoners.

"*Baruch Hashem*, we have been saved!" were the first words uttered by the Klausenberger upon his liberation. Later, he said,

"If the Master of the Universe in His great compassion and mercy has saved me from death, from this moment onward, I am obligated to dedicate my life to Him and His honor."

Afterwards, when the Rebbe learned that not a single member of his family had survived, his response was, "I have lost everything. But I have not lost Hashem."

Life in the DP Camps

The survivors were taken by train to a displaced persons camp in Feldafing, Germany, a town near Munich which was under American control. This became the Rebbe's home for the next six months, until his move to the larger camp of Foehrenwald.

The survivors brought to the DP camp were walking skeletons, all in a state of complete physical deterioration. Many who had survived the years of Nazi oppression collapsed upon liberation, falling into deep depression and losing the will to live. More than a few declared that they would have been better off dying in a gas chamber.

Yet the Rebbe, even in those first few difficult days, took charge of the situation. His lips trembled from weakness and suffering, but his eyes shone with an extraordinary light as he announced, "We are alive because we are Jews and we were commanded by Hashem to 'choose life!'"

Almost immediately he became the undisputed leader and spokesman for all the survivors living in the DP camp, a role he filled for the next year and a half until his move to America.

Early Priorities

The Rebbe's first priority in Feldafing was to bury the dead. The area surrounding the camp was littered with the corpses of Jews who had either been killed by the Nazis or died of starvation. Within a few days of liberation, the Rebbe had approached the DP camp commanders and requested that a car and a driver be assigned to him for the purpose of collecting the corpses and bringing them to the area set aside for burial.

These burial efforts lasted for several weeks and involved great danger, but this did not deter the Rebbe in the least. He established a burial society and instructed that Kaddish be recited for each person buried.

In addition to gathering up the dead for burial, the Rebbe also traveled to all the towns around Feldafing searching for fellow Jews who had survived the war by hiding in attics and underground bunkers. Many of these survivors thought that Hitler had exterminated the entire Jewish people and that there was no hope of ever resuming Jewish lives. Knowing this, the Rebbe went from town to town, seeking out Jews and bringing them back to the DP camps with him.

The Rebbe also turned his attention to the dozens of young orphans living in the camp who had no one to look out for them. Taking them under his wing, he involved himself in their spiritual needs and became a surrogate father to hundreds.

She'eiris HaPleitah

The lives of the survivors in the DP camp were organized by several central organizations which operated mainly in Munich,

Bergen-Belsen, and Berlin. Unfortunately, these organizations were all controlled by irreligious and Zionist factions.

As soon as he had recovered some of his strength, the Rebbe recognized the need to establish a network of organizations that would attend to the needs of the religious Jews in the camps. This network, which included both Torah institutions and general social and welfare institutions, was called "She'eiris HaPleitah."

The Rebbe did his utmost to acquire food and clothing for the penniless survivors. Appealing to Jews around the world and to government officials, he succeeded in bettering the physical as well as spiritual lives of the people in the camps.

As the father of all the orphans in the DP camps, the Rebbe also viewed it his personal obligation to establish a yeshivah and elementary school for young survivors. He obtained *sefarim* from American Jewish aid organizations, among them Vaad Hatzalah, and set up a dormitory and meals. Despite his overwhelmingly busy schedule, the Rebbe himself taught regular daily classes in Gemara and *Shulchan Aruch*. The Rebbe educated his students to live a life of Torah and fear of the Almighty, eventually seeing many of them to the marriage canopy.

He also opened a Bais Yaakov for refugee girls who came to Foehrenwald from all over Germany. In a very short time the school grew to five grades, with a student body of some 250 girls. The Rebbe was a father figure to these hundreds of girls, providing them with a warm Jewish home in which they could recover both physically and spiritually from the war.

These efforts were the beginning of what became the Rebbe's lifelong mission — rebuilding — first in the DP camps, then in America and finally in Eretz Yisrael.

Chapter 1

In a Barren Land

On Behalf of the Almighty and His People

After Pesach of 1946, the Rebbe decided to travel to America to raise funds for the destitute religious community in the DP camps and to explore the options for emigration from Germany. He spent seven weeks in New York, during which he touched the hearts of American Jews with his stirring prayer and awe-inspiring *tisches*. Working tirelessly and speaking endlessly about the survivors' plight, he succeeded in raising $100,000, a huge sum in those days.

After returning to Germany for a short time, the Rebbe prepared to leave for the United States again to pave the way for his followers' and students' immigration. When these intentions became known, one of the Rebbe's followers expressed disappointment that the Rebbe was immigrating to the United States and not to Eretz Yisrael. In a historic statement, the Rebbe responded, "I am traveling to Eretz Yisrael by way of the United States."

Later the Rebbe explained that he had given considerable thought to whether the United States or Eretz Yisrael would be a better place for him to serve the Almighty. Realizing that Eretz Yisrael already had many great chassidic rebbes, while America was a spiritually barren land that was in dire need of leadership, he decided to move to America for the time being, temporarily shelving his dream of moving to the Holy Land.

From his first day on American shores, at the end of Kislev 1946, the Klausenberger dedicated himself to the cause of disseminating Torah. Just as he had vowed to do while he was in Nazi captivity, he devoted himself completely to the Almighty and His people. In his first letter to his students still in Germany, the Rebbe wrote, "Before I rested from the difficulty of the journey, I began my work. With Hashem's help, and in the merit of our holy ancestors and the Torah study of young children, I am hopeful and confident that Hashem will enable me to succeed in my efforts and to raise the banner of Torah and Judaism."

First Steps on New Soil

As soon as the Rebbe arrived in New York, on Friday, 27 Kislev (the third night of Chanukah), he immediately set out for the temporary apartment that had been set up for him at 316 S. Fifth Street in Williamsburg. A group of young Holocaust survivors, who became the nucleus of Yeshivas Reishis Chochmah, the first yeshivah established by the Rebbe in America, also lived in the apartment at the time.

In this temporary apartment, the Klausenberger lit his Chanukah candles in the presence of several followers. Afterwards, on Shabbos, the apartment housed the Rebbe's minyan and *tisches*, which were attended by large crowds.

The Rebbe always conducted himself in his own unique manner, and this was true regarding his apartment, as well. An attractive apartment had been prepared for him on the second floor of the building, and the less attractive first floor of the building had been set aside as the *beis midrash*, a common practice in Williamsburg at that time. The Rebbe, however, proclaimed that it should be the exact opposite: "One can live even in a desolate hole, but to have such a *beis midrash*...?!" He therefore instructed that the *beis midrash* be moved to the larger, nicer room on the second floor and that his apartment be set up in the plainer room on the first floor. Even with respect to temporary quarters, he explained, "we must beautify the house of G-d."

An Urgent Rescue Mission

As the first influx of Holocaust survivors and refugees began to arrive in America, volunteers from the Joint Distribution Committee and HIAS greeted them at the port, offering to take the immigrants to boarding houses and other institutions under their auspices, where they would guide them in their decisions of where to settle in the new land. Both committees felt it would be best to settle the survivors in cities all across the country, so that they could integrate as quickly as possible into the local population. In their opinion, the large concentration of Jews in existence in New York at the time was an unhealthy phenomenon.

The Rebbe, of course, was of the exact opposite opinion. One of his primary missions was to point all immigrants in the direction of Williamsburg, which was already an established religious neighborhood, since he was convinced that living in any other environment would lead to spiritual destruction.

Two young orphans had come to America on the Rebbe's boat and were taken by the Joint to one of its absorption centers in the Bronx. Immediately after Shabbos, the Rebbe summoned one of his main assistants, a young man named Yosef Williger, and instructed him to go to the Bronx at once and do whatever he could to remove the two boys from the Joint's orphanage. "Bring them to me," he instructed.

Removing the boys from the clutches of the irreligious trustees of the Joint was no easy task. When the boys requested permission to leave the institution, they were forced to sign a statement waiving any financial support that had been collected on their behalf by the UNRWA, the United Nations refugee organization. This was very difficult for them. However, the Rebbe promised them that he would personally provide for all their needs, and encouraged them to join the other boys studying in his yeshivah. "Any place in America that is outside of the four cubits of halachah is *treife*," he warned them.

From then on, whenever the Rebbe heard of a boat of immigrants arriving from Europe, he would immediately dispatch special messengers to the port to tell the immigrants the true objectives of the Joint and HIAS representatives. At the same time, they would offer to take the immigrants to the Rebbe, who would provide them with comfortable temporary living quarters and help them acclimate to their new lives.

A Focus on the Klal

The Klausenberger never spent even a minute thinking about himself or about his own personal life. Even after his arrival in America, his thoughts were focused first and foremost on one critical question: How could he expedite getting physical and spiritual assistance to the displaced persons that were left behind in Germany? As before, the Rebbe was most worried about the spiritual futures of the young orphans who turned to him for guidance. He never stopped searching for ways to get these children out of the blood-soaked soil of Europe. As his efforts began to bear fruit, he turned his energies to preparing a spiritual refuge for them in America.

At the same time, the Rebbe also worked to raise money and obtain religious articles for the Orthodox communities of Romania and Transylvania, which were trying to rebuild themselves after the Holocaust. In a letter to the Joint Distribution Committee on 19 Shevat, 5707 (1947), the Rebbe demanded that the Committee immediately send the resources necessary to reestablish Jewish life in these areas.

"The terrible destruction of North Transylvanian Jewry is all too well known," he wrote. "Synagogues and yeshivos in every one of these 106 communities have been completely destroyed. Religious articles of every type were brutally torn apart, burned, and destroyed by cruel and wicked people... The yeshivos that exist now were organized and established anew with extraordinary selflessness... These communities have no *sifrei Torah* or *sifrei Tanach, mishnayos,* or Gemaras, no mezuzos, tefillin, *taleisim,* or siddurim... You must fill this lack immediately."

"One Must Be a Revolutionary"

In addition to his activities on behalf of the *she'eiris*

hapleitah, the Rebbe was also concerned from the start with the second and third generation American Jews, who were unfortunately drifting far from their heritage. With his broad vision, the Klausenberger saw a vast expanse of barren land that needed to be worked. The words of his colleague Rabbi Shraga Feivel Mendelowitz reverberated in his mind: "In order to act on behalf of the Almighty and His Torah in America, one must be a revolutionary. Otherwise there is no hope."

"First we must be concerned with the Jews who know only the verse '*Shema Yisrael*,' to save them from spiritual destruction. Then we can turn our attention to the Jews who also recite the verse '*Ve'ahavta es Hashem Elokecha*,' " he would say.

Spiritual Desolation

The spiritual state of American Jewry at the time can be seen clearly in the following story:

One of the descendants of the Divrei Chaim of Sanz who had survived the Holocaust but had lost his entire family in the war approached the Rebbe one day with an agonizing question: "I know that I am getting older and will not live much longer," he said. "I may not have enough years left to raise my children in the ways of the Torah, and I see that here in America it is very difficult to raise children who remain faithful to the Torah. In such a situation, is it proper for me to remarry? Perhaps it is better not to have children at all in this land!"

Echoing the words of the Prophet Yeshayah to King Chizkiyahu, who posed a similar question when he was told that he would father a son who would be an evildoer and lead the Jewish people astray, the Rebbe responded, "This is not your concern. Your obligation is to marry and observe Hashem's command."

One writer accurately portrayed the Rebbe's greatness in the following manner: "If Reb Shraga Feivel Mendelowitz laid the foundation of *Yiddishkeit* in America and Rav Aharon Kotler built the walls and the roof, it was the Klausenberger Rebbe who gave it its soul."

Purely for the Sake of Heaven

When the Rebbe arrived in America, he made a decision that he would not derive any physical pleasure from that land. As a close follower of his attested, "In twenty-five years, I never saw the Rebbe ever doing anything for himself — everything was for the sake of Heaven. All his worries and efforts were completely for *kevod Shamayim* and for the sake of *klal Yisrael*."

In one lecture, the Rebbe revealed one of the reasons that he was so committed to strengthening the spiritual lives of others. "We see that when Moshe Rabbeinu at first refused to accept the leadership of the Jewish people, Hashem told him to throw his staff on the ground, and it became a snake. Hashem was demonstrating to Moshe that even a simple Jew, if his *rav* and spiritual guide does not hold on to him firmly, will fall to the ground and turn into a poisonous snake. Then Hashem said to Moshe, 'Stretch out your hand and hold onto its tail'; meaning that even if he turns into a snake, if the rebbe holds onto him properly from his tail, where he does not bite, the person will return and become a faithful Jew once again.

'And what if someone says, 'Why do I need this trouble? Isn't it better for me to seclude myself and study Torah day and night and be concerned only with my own spirituality?' Regarding this the Almighty said to Moshe, 'Put your hand in your bosom,' and Moshe was instantly afflicted with *tzara'as*. This teaches us that if a tzaddik does not help others and only looks out for himself, he will eventually become afflicted himself, for one is never free of his obligation to help others with their spiritual needs."

The Rebbe also often used to relate his own insight into the verses in *Nitzavim*: "Lest there is among you a man or woman or a family or tribe whose heart turns away today from Hashem, our G-d... And he blesses himself in his heart, saying, 'Peace will be with me, though I walk as my heart sees fit...' Hashem will not be willing to forgive him" (*Devarim* 29:17–19). The Klausenberger asked, "It would seem that we are talking about an evil person who has turned his back on Hashem. Why should he care if Hashem does not forgive him?

"This *pasuk*," he explained, "can be understood on a different level. It speaks not of an evil person, but rather of a tzaddik! For there are some tzaddikim who say to themselves, 'Peace will be with me – I will look out only for my own peace of mind; and therefore I will walk as my heart sees fit – I will deal only with my own spirituality, and I will not be concerned with anyone else's situation.' To such a person Hashem delivers an ominous warning – He will not be willing to forgive him."

The Sanz Yeshivah

At the end of the summer of 1946, shortly before the Rebbe returned to Europe after his first visit to America, the Rebbe appointed Rav Aharon Yehudah Wilner to teach Gemara to the *bachurim* of the Sanzer Kloiz and Rav Moshe Zev Lieber to take care of their physical needs. A new group of young men who emigrated from Germany with the Rebbe joined this group. More *bachurim* joined the yeshivah over the course of the winter, thanks to affidavits that the Rebbe obtained for them from Rabbi Shraga Feivel Mendelowitz of Mesivta Torah Vodaas, and before long the Sanz Yeshivah comprised a large group of students who learned Torah and lived an authentic chassidic life. The yeshivah's quarters soon became too crowded and additional rooms and apartments were rented to house the growing number of students. Later, the Rebbe purchased a new building on Rodney Street, and the yeshivah moved there.

The Sanz Yeshivah was the first classic chassidic yeshivah established in America. Many people tried to discourage the Rebbe from establishing such a yeshivah, saying that it would never succeed: "Only when hair grows on our palms will a chassidic yeshivah flourish in America!" The Rebbe refused to pay attention to these arguments. In later years, he would say jokingly, "I want to see them today. Perhaps hair has started to grow on their palms!"

The yeshivah became a magnet both for Holocaust survivors who had become close to the Rebbe in the DP camps and for the children of chassidic families that had already settled in America. More rebbeim were hired, including Rav Yerachmiel Yisrael Yitzchak Skula, the Sadubna Rav, and Rabbi Yitzchak Yehudah Stern of Bilitz.

The following account, printed in a local newspaper, describes the celebratory event held at the yeshivah to mark the start of a new winter *zeman*:

Most yeshivos in America have a celebratory ceremony at the

conclusion of the year of study. The Klausenberg Yeshivah [however] follows the custom of traditional Hungarian yeshivos and celebrates the beginning of the *zeman*...

Around the table sat the important and honored members of the religious community of Williamsburg... There was the Rav of Tzehlem, the Kopishnitzer Rebbe, the Spinka Rebbe, the Rav of Miskolc, the *rosh yeshivah* Rav Aharon Yehudah Wilner, the *rosh mesivta* Rav Williger, and many others.

In the center sat the guest of honor, the Klausenberger Rebbe — an extraordinary person, known for his superhuman rescue efforts after the Holocaust... Tens of students present at the celebration in the yeshivah's hall, together with the hundreds of visitors who came for the event, were living testimony to the awesome accomplishments of this great man. Survivors of both physical and spiritual destruction, they followed the Rebbe's every movement with bated breath and absorbed every sound he uttered. The Rebbe stepped onto the platform next to the *aron kodesh*... Trembling, he kissed the *paroches*, paused for a few seconds as he whispered words of prayer, and then opened the *Chumash* that was on the lectern before him and began to expound on Torah reading of the week, *Parashas Lech Lecha*.

"You know," he said to his audience, "that some regard Noach in an unfavorable light because he was not concerned with the people of his generation. Noach was a pure, righteous man, but all his righteousness was for himself. Our forefather Avraham, on the other hand, excelled as the pillar of compassion and kindness in both material matters and spiritual matters...

"Indeed," continued the Rebbe, "it is not enough to establish a yeshivah and gather young people to learn on the benches of the *beis midrash*. We must also watch over them day and night and protect them from the evil influences of the times...so that the age-old spirit of *Yiddishkeit* is preserved in them, just as in generations of old. Alas, how much *siyatta diShmaya* we need, so that we do not fall prey to the dangerous trap that is America."

With these last words, the Rebbe let out a deep groan, a groan that echoed through the entire auditorium.

With the Purest of Approaches

The Rebbe was firm in his conviction that the yeshivah be guided in the purest fashion and that it not be influenced to the slightest degree, by the atmosphere of the times. He forbade the teaching of English in the yeshivah; rather, students who wanted to learn English had to go to a one-hour evening course at Mesivta Torah Vodaas. He also did not allow the yeshivah to give its graduates *semichah*, as was customary in American yeshivos. "My goal is not to establish a factory for rabbis, but rather to create a *makom Torah* where the students learn solely *l'sheim shamayim*," he would often say.

When one of the students of the yeshivah came to the Rebbe one day and confided that his parents were about to come fight with the Rebbe because he would not allow their son to go to college, the Rebbe responded calmly that he was not afraid of them at all.

He told the student, "A certain sharp *rav* was approached by a man who had written a commentary on *Sefer Mishlei* and wanted a *haskamah*. The *rav* examined the work and saw that it was not very good. He jokingly told the author, 'It would have been better if you'd have written a commentary on *Iyov*.'

"Surprised, the man asked, 'Why?'

"The *rav* answered, 'Iyov lived a life of trials and tribulations. One more tribulation like your commentary would not have affected his difficult situation at all. Shlomo HaMelech, however, lived most of his days in great comfort and wealth. Why should you make him suffer with your commentary?'

"So it is with me," the Rebbe continued. "I am used to suffering and difficulty of all types. Problems do not faze me. We will deal with them, *b'ezras Hashem*."

The Rosh Yeshivah

The Rebbe regarded the *rosh yeshivah*, Rav Aharon Yehudah Wilner, as a "living *sefer*," "a master of the entire Talmud," who "knew every *Tosafos* in *Shas* by heart," and "had amazing insights into every page of the Talmud." Reb Aharon Yehudah served as the head of the yeshivah for over forty years.

Reb Aharon Yehudah was the nephew and *talmid muvhak* of the famous Torah giant Rav Meir Arak, author of the *Imrei Yosher* and one of the greatest *poskim* in Galicia in the previous generation. His entire personality had been molded by his uncle's teachings.

As a child, he had been orphaned of both parents. His uncle, Rav Meir Arak, took him in and became both his father and his teacher. When Rav Meir Arak was forced to flee his home in

Boteshta during World War I, he took his nephew with him to Vienna. Out of his fondness for his nephew, Rav Meir Arak included in several of his *sefarim* insights that he heard from his brilliant young student.

In a letter of approbation which he wrote for his nephew in 1919, Reb Meir referred to his young student in glowing terms: "My nephew, who calls wisdom his sister, is a sharp witted and outstanding student," he wrote. "He is a senior student who has reached the level of instruction, and his brilliance and memory are truly exceptional. He has studied various tractates and the laws of the *Shulchan Aruch* with me and is an expert in them. They are set and concealed in his heart and lips. His diligence in the study of Torah is awe-inspiring, and all his desires lies in it."

In the certificate of ordination that he gave Reb Aharon Yehudah three years later, in 1922, Reb Meir Arak noted that his nephew was "sharp-witted and knowledgeable in all aspects of Torah. He is a precious vessel that retains everything. His vision of the Talmud and codifiers is crystal clear, and he has mastered the area of practical instruction as well. Any subject to which he turns his attention he not only understands but also masters with clarity."

Expansive knowledge and deep insight were Reb Aharon Yehudah's trademarks throughout his life. He was an outstanding *masmid* and never wasted a moment of time. (He would often recall, "My uncle Reb Meir would say that in the time when the rest of the world slept, he managed to learn the entire *Shas* four times.") Everything that he learned was organized in his mind in a clear and concise fashion. He would review everything he learned again and again, time after time, with great thirst, as if he had just begun to learn Torah. Twice a year he completed the entire Talmud with commentaries, *rishonim* and *acharonim* alike, whose words he could recite entirely from memory. He was also fluent in books of Aggadah and Chassidus and in commentaries on Tanach.

The Rebbe related several times that he had chosen Reb Aharon Yehudah as *rosh yeshivah* mainly because his entire essence served as a role model of a genuine Torah personality. Equally important to the Rebbe was Reb Aharon Yehudah's significant contribution in molding the *middos* and personalities of the students of the Sanz Yeshivah. Years later, when a group of the yeshivah's students moved to Eretz Yisrael to learn in Netanyah, the Rebbe would say, "If I were to discuss a *sugya* with the *talmidim*, I can tell immediately which has learned from Reb Aharon Yehudah. His mark is evident on those who learned from him."

Reb Aharon Yehudah was both modest and humble. He nullified himself completely before the Rebbe and brought all his questions to him. The Rebbe accorded Reb Aharon Yehudah with the utmost respect, and would rise from his chair in honor of the *rosh yeshivah* even when he was weak and ill.

Reb Aharon Yehudah never desired anything for himself and did not allow his students to serve him in the simplest of ways. He greeted everyone, even the youngest child, with warmth and love.

Only on rare occasions would Reb Aharon Yehudah talk about himself. On one very rainy day in Union City, he told a student about a time in his youth in Germany, when he learned for six hours straight on a very cold day, without realizing that his legs were frozen. Only when he took a short break from his studies and tried to stand did he realize that he could not move his legs. On another occasion, he found his students studying *Bava Metzia* and asked them what they did on the long summer Friday afternoons. He then related that in his youth when these long Shabbosos arrived he would spend eight or nine hours studying the tractate of *Bava Metzia* all the way until the *sugya* of *Kol HaNishum*, which they were presently learning.

"Even if I was paid a million dollars to sit for a minute and do nothing, I cannot," he once told a student. When he was badly injured in a car accident, he related afterwards that his main concern was whether he had suffered from any loss of memory. He immediately began to mentally check his own memory and to review in his mind entire pages of the Ramban (he had written a *sefer* on Rambam's commentary on *Shas*), until he was sure that his memory had not been affected. Only then did he calm down.

Even in his later years Reb Aharon Yehudah's thought processes were still sharp and clear. He was completely energized by and lived for Torah. When he passed away on Monday, 11 Elul, 1986, his essence was aptly captured by one of his eulogizers: "Reb Aharon Yehudah was the last of those truly devoted to the Torah."

On the day of his passing, the crown of Yeshivas She'eiris HaPleitah was taken.

Chapter 2

In the Tent of Torah

The Rebbe and His Talmidim

For approximately eight months after his arrival in America, the Klausenberger lived in the yeshivah building with his orphan students, living very simply and making do with very little. The door of his apartment was fitted with a clear glass window such that one could see into the apartment from the hallway. The boys were therefore able to see into the Klausenberger's apartment as they passed it on their way to their own dormitory rooms. This gave them the opportunity to observe how the Rebbe was always awake, learning intensely at a simple table day and night.

The Rebbe's personal conduct throughout this time was amazing to behold. Never was he seen sleeping or resting. Occasionally he was seen sitting and learning his feet in a pot of cold water so that he wouldn't fall asleep. Only the student who lived in the Rebbe's apartment with him slept on a bed (during the winter the Rebbe would cover the boy with his coat so he would not be cold) and almost every morning the Rebbe would ask this student to recite *Birchas HaTorah* on his behalf.

One night the Rebbe happened to be alone in his room all night and fell asleep for a few minutes shortly before dawn. When he awoke and realized what had happened, he didn't want to move from his chair without first washing his hands, so he dialed the number of the pay phone that was near the *beis midrash*. One of the *bachurim* answered the phone. Humbly identifying himself as "Zalman Leib," the Rebbe meekly requested a washing cup and some water to be brought to his room so that he could wash his hands.

Yet the Rebbe was not absorbed in his learning to the exclusion of all else. He would often leave his room in the middle of the night to check on the sleeping *bachurim* in the dormitory. He would replace fallen blankets and cover sleeping students as if he was caring for his own children. Occasionally he would bring a basin and a cup of water to the bedside of a student who had forgotten to prepare them for himself. When a *bachur* was sick, the Rebbe would bring him medicine and hot tea. He would go to the dormitory rooms early in the morning to wake the *bachurim* so they could learn for a few hours before *shacharis*, telling them jokingly, "I can already hear the wheels of the subway, and you are still sleeping?"

The Rebbe did whatever was necessary to keep the yeshivah functioning. When the *bachurim* went to eat breakfast, he would take a broom and sweep the floor of the *beis midrash*. On fast days he would walk through the *beis midrash* to see how the *bachurim* were feeling. If he saw a *bachur* who looked pale, he would instruct him to go to the kitchen and break his fast.

Fasting for Himself and for Others

The Rebbe himself was careful to observe all fast days, and in fact took extra fast days on himself. During the period of Shovevim the Rebbe fasted all day, and only at night would he eat a little. However, these fasts were kept secret. Even after the Klausenberger remarried, his *rebbetzin* did not know anything about his fasting. Every day she would bring the Rebbe a cup of coffee after he had finished davening. The Rebbe, however, would find something that required his attention and delay drinking the coffee without telling her why. On these fast days, the Rebbe would remain in his tallis and tefillin until late in the day, when he davened *minchah*. Then he would recite *maariv*, and only then eat and drink a little.

Reb Nesanel Tzvi Wax, one of the Klausenberger's assistants during his early years in America, recalled another incident: A fire once broke out in a She'eris HaPleitah building on a Friday morning of the week of *Parashas Chukas*. The Rebbe was told about the fire after *shacharis*. He asked about the extent of the damage and Reb Nesanel Tzvi told him. As the Rebbe was contemplating the monetary value of the damage and considering the adequacy of the yeshivah's insurance, he suddenly fell deep in thought. Finally, he roused himself and said, "Today is Friday of *Parashas Chukas*, a day on which some have the custom to fast over the burning of the Torah."

"The next year," Reb Nesanel Tzvi added, "I made certain to observe the Rebbe on that day and I saw that he was indeed fasting."

His Connection to His Talmidim

One night a *bachur* in the yeshivah dormitory lit the gas on the stove to boil water for coffee and forgot to turn it off. The gas soon spread to the dormitory rooms, where other *bachurim* were sleeping. Three *bachurim* lost consciousness and were rushed to the hospital.

When the Klausenberger heard what had occurred, he was aghast. Just hearing the words *gas poisoning* made him start to shake. Without saying a word, he went into his apartment, closed the door behind him, and did not allow anyone in. No one knew what he was doing, but it was clear that he was busy in ways known only to himself, trying to arouse mercy for the injured boys.

Three hours later, the Rebbe emerged from his room and asked whether there was any news from the hospital. When he was told that the boys had regained consciousness and seemed to be doing well, he was finally able to relax.

An Erev Pesach Mitzvah

On *erev Pesach* 1947, the Rebbe succeeded, with great effort, in organizing a late-afternoon matzah baking, as was his custom. The baking took place in a building on the Lower East Side of Manhattan. When the Rebbe returned home after the baking was done, he noticed that *yom tov* meals had not yet been prepared for the yeshivah students. Immediately, he entered the kitchen, picked up a knife, and began to peel potatoes.

The others with him were stunned. "Should the Rebbe become a cook?" they asked in horror.

The Rebbe answered them simply, "And if I do? Is baking matzos more important than feeding a *ben Torah* is?" Then he added jokingly, "And if you feel that this task is inappropriate for me, why don't you give me a hand?"

Attempts to Earn a Livelihood

In the first days after his arrival in America, the Rebbe tried to find himself a source of income that was not connected to the holy work in which he was immersed day and night. His great wish to earn his livelihood with his own hands, so that he could devote himself to disseminating Torah on a purely altruistic basis, without a hint of personal gain. As he wrote in a letter later published in the *sefer Shefa Chaim*, "If I could do what I wanted to...and I had a way to earn a livelihood from my own labors like I have here, with the help of the Almighty, I would flee on the wings of eagles to our holy land and see its beauty and its rebuilding..." Similarly, at the beginning of the summer *zeman* in the yeshivah in 1981, the Rebbe noted, "It is some forty years that I have not taken any remuneration from the community."

Without any concern over his own stature or his honor, the Rebbe decided to learn diamond cutting, a trade common among many Jews in Brooklyn at the time. However, he soon realized that this was not a vocation that suited him because he would often begin to ponder spiritual matters while he was working. Filled with lofty thoughts of *deveikus* to Hashem, he would lose concentration, take his eye off the stones in the drill, and damage the stones. He was therefore forced to stop learning this trade.

The Rebbe then attempted to open a Jewish bookstore. This, too, proved unsuccessful, and he eventually abandoned the idea.

"It Is Time to Focus on the Yeshivah"

The Rebbe experienced many challenges and obstacles in his first few years in the United States. In a letter to his dear friend Rav Avraham Getzel Shiff, he wrote in a heartfelt fashion how at first he thought, "At last those who believe in G-d and His holy Torah will give me a little help." He decided to emigrate to America, where "I thought that my burden would be eased, so that I would be better able to carry it."

But the reality was precisely the opposite. "Everyone is concerned with their own personal situation, and there is no one to get involved." "Were it not for some followers of my father who have supported me with great *mesiras nefesh*," he continued, "She'eiris HaPleitah would have, G-d forbid, already sunk completely. But I am concerned for the honor of the Almighty and the honor of religious Jewry, and I am working day and night to pay its many obligations and to save what can be saved."

As time passed and it became clear to the Klausenberger that the main task of the She'eiris HaPleitah organization in Germany was finished, since most of the displaced persons had already emigrated to their new homes — thanks to the Rebbe's efforts in obtaining visas for them — he told his secretary, Reb Mordechai Taub, "From now on we will focus entirely on the yeshivah, for it is a small thing that will sustain my soul!"

From that day onward, the Klausenberger focused most of his efforts on the welfare of the yeshivah body, which numbered almost one hundred. His deep desire was to provide for them properly, both spiritually and materially. He davened with them every day, both morning and evening. Between *minchah* and *maariv*, he gave a *shiur* in *Shulchan Aruch HaRav*, focusing on the laws of Talmud Torah. This was in addition to the complex *shiurim* he gave from time to time on Gemara and *rishonim*. He also gave a *shiur* on the laws of Shabbos each Friday and a *shiur* on *Choshen Mishpat* on one of the weekdays in his home.

At the same time, the Rebbe also put his energies into raising the funds necessary to support the students. He assembled a group of individuals to serve as a board to assist him in this effort, among them was Reb Nechemyah Karn, Reb Baruch Frankel, and Reb Moshe Rosenberg.

At one point the Rebbe even considered setting up an agricultural farm near the yeshivah to be run by former *talmidim* who were now married, so that they could earn an honest living in a proper environment, with a portion of their profits going to help support the yeshivah. However, for a variety of reasons this idea never came to fruition.

A Machatzis HaShekel

The Rebbe would not take a penny from the funds he collected for his own personal needs. His financial situation was such that when Purim approached, he did not even have enough money to give the customary half-shekel for *tzedakah* before the megillah reading.

The next day, when Reb Shaul Paszkes brought the Rebbe a *mishloach manos* with a cake inside, the Rebbe asked him to buy back the cake. With the money Reb Shaul gave him the Rebbe was able to follow the custom of giving *tzedakah* on Purim as a remembrance of the *machatzis hashekel*.

The Value of a Bit of Teshuvah

Despite his dire need of funds, the Rebbe refused to give honor where it was not deserved and never ingratiated himself to anyone. There was one very wealthy man who contributed vast sums to many yeshivos in America and was viewed in high-regard. One day, he was brought to meet the Rebbe in the hopes that he would become a supporter of the She'eiris HaPleitah institutions.

The Klausenberger began to converse with the man and inquired, with great interest, about his health and his various activities. The philanthropist innocently told the Rebbe that his business was so successful that it no longer required much of his time to manage. Instead, he was free to spend his time traveling, vacationing, and playing cards.

Hearing this, the Rebbe rebuked the man, "You are already seventy-five years old, and you should be thinking about your *neshamah* and about what awaits it in the World to Come! You are a believer in Hashem, in reward and punishment. Remember well where you will be going and before Whom you will have to give an accounting of your life's activities..."

At first, the Rebbe's rebuke was gentle, but as he continued to speak his tone became more strident. "Do you think that because of your charitable contributions you will be seated in Gan Eden with all the righteous of Israel? You are making a grave error! You will be brought to judgment for every minute of life that you waste! In fact, because you contributed money that you won in card games to yeshivos, you are very likely to be judged to Gehinnom, because this money was used to feed students who are learning Torah. Since the money comes from impure sources, their hearts and minds have been sullied and they cannot learn properly. You will be responsible for this!"

The wealthy benefactor left the Rebbe angry and humiliated. No one had ever spoken to him in such a manner. Of course, the matter of a contribution to the She'eiris HaPleitah institutions was completely forgotten. The Rebbe's followers were very upset. They simply could not understand why the Rebbe had suddenly decided to alienate the wealthy Jew.

The Rebbe, seeing their distress and astonishment, hastened to explain: "Do I need any money for myself? Of course not. I only accept money from people in order to increase the honor of the Almighty and to glorify the Torah. As such, how can I be concerned only with the welfare of the *yeshivah bachurim*? Do I have no responsibility for the welfare of a lost Jew like this one, who is wasting his time on this earth with emptiness?

"I do not fool myself that even after a rebuke such as this he will immediately change his ways," continued the Rebbe, "But if until now he was likely to end his life believing that he would be going straight to Gan Eden, perhaps at least now there is a chance that in the final moments of his life he will have pangs of regret and do *teshuvah*. This arousal is worth more to me than all the money that we could have received from him."

Full-Time Torah Learning

The Klausenberger also made sure that his *talmidim*, who were his adopted children, made Torah study their full-time occupation. Anyone who learned in the yeshivah was prohibited from obtaining part-time employment, even if it did not involve leaving the yeshivah during set study times. Rather, the Rebbe insisted that they devote their full energies to Torah study and *avodas Hashem*.

It was common practice in these days for young men to go out into the world and learn a trade. As a result, many young Jews were influenced by the secular American society and seduced by its spiritually destructive atmosphere. The Klausenberger fought this practice vigorously. Even when it came to a boy whose father was a main supporter of the Rebbe, the Klausenberger not change his policy and told the father firmly, "If your son goes to work, you may also leave the *beis midrash*."

The Klausenberger also promised the *yeshivah bachurim* that he would personally provide for their material needs, arrange their *shidduchim*, including living expenses and wedding expenses, and even arrange a livelihood for them after their weddings.

When it came to the Rebbe's adopted "children," the Holocaust survivors that he had brought to America from the DP camps, the Klausenberger involved himself in their *shidduchim* just like a father. His name appeared on the wedding invitations and he officiated at every wedding ceremony. He would dance at every *mitzvah tantz* with as much joy and enthusiasm as a biological parent. The students in turn felt like they were his children, and remained close to him even as the years passed.

A Personal Assurance

One of the outstanding *talmidim* of the yeshivah once came

to the Klausenberger and related to him with great concern that he might have to look for temporary employment in order to pay for some major dental work that his widowed mother needed desperately. The Rebbe immediately gave the student the entire amount necessary so that he not take his mind off his learning even for a short time.

When one of the *yeshivah bachurim* succumbed to the pressures of the times and went to work part time, the Klausenberger did not allow him to remain in the yeshivah, even though he continued to learn part time, because he was afraid of the influence he might have on others in the yeshivah. One day, the Rebbe met the young man in question on the street. The former *talmid* wanted to accompany the Rebbe on his way, but the Rebbe refused, saying, "After all, you aren't going in my direction."

On another occasion the Rebbe tried to convince a top *bachur* who had left the yeshivah to return to his learning. He used all kinds of strategies to accomplish this and even warned the young man that he was causing great pain to his deceased father. He gave the young man his personal assurance that if he returned to Torah study his life would be ever pleasant. Eventually, the young man returned to full-time learning for another two years.

"Those two years were the best years of my life," he admitted many years later.

An Absolute Condition

One of the Rebbe's most devoted students recalled the following: "I came to America in 1948, together with two of my friends. We had all learned in Yeshivas Meor HaGolah, under the auspices of Reb Yaakov Lechovitzky, in Rome. When we arrived in Williamsburg, we went straight to Yeshivas She'eiris HaPleitah. The Klausenberger was not feeling well that day and could not come out to greet us. Instead, he welcomed us in his room, lying on his bed. He shook our hands in greeting and then sent us to the *beis midrash* to hear Rav Wilner's *shiur*, which made a great impression upon us.

"Later that day, when we asked to be accepted into the yeshivah, we were told that we needed the Klausenberger's personal approval for this. We went to the Rebbe's room a second time and requested permission to stay. The Rebbe looked at us very intensely, evaluating us, and said, 'I see that you are older, and you will surely soon get married. You must be honest with yourselves: Are you willing to give up everything and devote yourselves entirely to Torah? If you go to work, you may be able to earn a lot of money and save money for marriage. If you are accepted into the yeshivah, however, you may cause pain to both of us, since we do not allow any *bachurim* to remain unless they are only learning.' "

The three young *bachurim* did indeed decide to stay, and they merited to serve the Rebbe for many years.

Making a Shidduch

There was an older *bachur* in the yeshivah who was having difficulty finding a match. His concerned friends felt that this was because he was not earning a living. They therefore advised him, "You should learn a trade and be seen as a breadwinner, and then everyone will be jumping at you."

This advice threw the *bachur* into a state of total confusion.

He knew well the Rebbe's view that his *talmidim* should not go to work before getting married, and did not dare ask the Rebbe what to do. Finally, he shared his pain with a close friend who offered to accompany him to the Rebbe to discuss the matter.

Together, the two young men went to the Klausenberger, and the *bachur*'s friend presented the dilemma. The Rebbe asked him sharply, "Are you his guardian?"

The young man sheepishly explained that his friend was very shy and was afraid to discuss the subject with the Rebbe.

Turning to the older *bachur,* the Rebbe said, "You should know, my son, that we have total faith in all the words of our Sages, without exception. Not a single thing that *Chazal* said is false, and if one does not believe this it is a sign that he is infected with the seeds of disbelief. Our Sages explicitly taught that forty days before a child is conceived, his mate is announced, and *Tosafos* explains that this is specifically before the conception of a boy. Therefore, you must ask yourself: Is it possible that someone who goes out into the corrupt street and is not careful with where his eyes wander will find his mate, while one who is careful with what he looks at will not? Heaven help us from such logic! Return to your place in the yeshivah, and Hashem will help you find a wife!"

Several days later, the Rebbe summoned the *bachur*'s friend and said to him with a smile, "You are his guardian, and you should know that they are already saying great things about him. However, since he is shy, as you said yourself, you must help him move things along. I promise that you will have *siyatta diShmaya* in this endeavor!"

And so it was.

The Rebbe's Remarriage

On *erev Shabbos Parashas Shoftim*, the sixth of Elul 1947, the Klausenberger married his second wife, the righteous Rebbetzin Chaya Nechama, the daughter of the saintly *gaon* Rav Shmuel Dovid Ungar, author of *Neos Desheh* and head of the Nitra *beis din*, who had been one of the *gedolei hador* in Europe before the Holocaust.

The wedding was held in the Nitra Yeshivah, which was located in Somerville, New Jersey. The Rebbe walked to the *chuppah* wrapped in a tallis, his face glowing, escorted by Rav Dovid Tzvi Halberstam of Kishinov. The day before the wedding, the Klausenberger called his chassidim in Germany and requested that all the She'eiris HaPleitah yeshivos arrange a festive meal for the *talmidim* in honor of his marriage, to be paid for by the Rebbe. That Friday night, after the wedding, the Rebbe conducted his customary public *tisch* as usual, without any change from his usual practice.

In honor of the marriage, Rav Levi Yitzchak Greenwald, the *rav* of Tzehlem and a great admirer of the Rebbe, wrote him the following letter:

Erev Rosh Chodesh Elul, 5707

...I was honored to receive the invitation to the Rav's wedding and day of great joy. I am unable to participate in this celebration, since I have the wedding of the orphaned daughter of Rav Dov Amsel on the same day, so I am sending my simple blessing now. May the honor of this house be greater than the one that preceded it and may the blessing of the elders to Boaz come to fruition, "May Hashem make the woman who comes to your house like Ra-

*chel and Leah, who built the House of Israel;" and may you merit
to rebuild the house of your holy ancestor, the Divrei Chaim,
which was destroyed as the result of our many sins, and may you
merit to see a pure and upright generation of blessing.*

*Your beloved friend, who is always concerned for your wel-
fare and awaits the salvation of all of the Jewish people,*

Levi Yitzchak ben Zissel

These blessings and good wishes were indeed fulfilled. The
Rebbe merited to rebuild anew the Sanz dynasty established by
the Divrei Chaim. The saintly Rebbetzin Chaya Nechama remained at the Rebbe's side for the next forty-seven years, until
the end of his life, and they were blessed with pure and holy offspring, all of whom followed in their parents' footsteps: two
sons, Rav Tzvi Elimelech and Rav Shmuel Dovid; and five
daughters, Rebbetzin Miriam Leah, wife of Rav Shlomo
Goldman, the Rebbe of Zvhil; Rebbetzin Chava Mindel, wife of
Rav Dov Weiss, head of the Sanz Beis Din in Jerusalem;
Rebbetzin Hinda Chana, wife of Rav Efrayim Fishel Mutzen, the
rav of Kiryat Besht in Petach Tikvah; Rebbetzin Yehudis, wife of
Rav Shaul Yehudah Prizant, *dayan* in Union City; and Rebbetzin
Sara Esther Basha, wife of Rav Eliezer Dovid Shapiro, a rebbe in
the Sanz Yeshivah in Netanyah.

"How Did I Merit This?"

Twenty-three years later, on Shabbos *Parashas Shoftim* at
the beginning of Elul 5730, at the *sheva berachos* of his oldest
son, Reb Tzvi Elimelech, the Rebbe spoke in public, with great
emotion, on the events of his life:

"Many times I have thought to myself and contemplated how the Creator has bestowed His mercy upon me after all the suffering which I experienced. I have merited to rebuild anew; I have been blessed with sons and sons-in-law who are Torah scholars; I have merited to establish a beautiful yeshivah that blossoms with Torah leaders and *yirei Shamayim*; and so much more.

"I stand in amazement and wonder, what good thing did I do that pleased the Almighty and caused Him to bless me so?

"I have reached the conclusion that the only thing I could possibly have done to merit all this is that even in the most difficult times I never once had a complaint against the Creator. Rather, with every wave that passed over me, threatening to drown me, I bowed my head and accepted it with love."

A Servant to His Master

After his marriage the Klausenberger lived for a short time in the home of Baruch Frankel. Afterwards, he moved into a rented apartment at 158 Rodney Street in Williamsburg, near the yeshivah, where he continued his daily and nightly schedule. Reb Yitzchak Ehrenreich, a close follower of the Klausenberger, related: "One night I was at the Rebbe's apartment until two in the morning. I asked the Rebbe in wonder, 'Why doesn't the Rebbe go to sleep?' He answered, 'How can I go to sleep when you are sitting here with me?' I immediately got up and left. An hour later, I thought to myself, 'Let me go and see what the Rebbe is doing.' I went back to the apartment and saw that the Rebbe was sitting in his place learning Torah, his eyes focused on the Gemara, reciting the text in a sweet melody. I stood there for a long time, unable to take my eyes off of this extraordinary sight."

Occasionally, the Rebbe would ask a student to sleep in his apartment so that he could awaken the Rebbe early in the morning. However, when the student would wake up he would always find the Rebbe already awake.

The Rebbe's dedicated personal secretary Reb Mordechai Taub, who came to Yeshivas She'eiris HaPleitah in the summer of 1947 and served as the Rebbe's assistant for the next ten years, came to greet the Rebbe one morning as he arrived for *shacharis*. They met on the way, and the Rebbe asked him, "Where are you going?" Reb Mordechai responded in Yiddish, "*A kegen dem Rebbe* (To greet the Rebbe)."

The Rebbe smiled and said good-naturedly (in a play on the word *kegen* which can also mean "against"), "Do not ever go against me."

The Rebbe lived in poverty after his marriage. The apartment was tiny, and the furniture broken and torn from old age and long use. The Skverer Rebbe, Rabbi Yaakov Yosef Twersky, *zt"l*, once visited the Rebbe in his apartment. The Rebbe gave him a chair to sit on, but when the Skverer Rebbe tried to sit down it became clear that the chair was broken. The Rebbe quickly switched chairs with his guest, giving him the chair that he had been sitting on.

The Skverer Rebbe refused to take the Rebbe's chair because he did not want him to sit on a broken chair. Only after the Rebbe begged his guest to use his chair did the Skverer Rebbe relent and sat down. Pointing to the broken and worn furniture, the Skverer Rebbe asked the Klausenberger in his usual terse style, "How can you live like this?"

The Rebbe responded, "A servant should not be better off than his master, and as long as Hashem's name is not complete, His throne is also not complete."

Like an Angel

A short time after his marriage, the Rebbe took ill and was hospitalized for several days. He asked his brother-in-law Rav Michel Ber Weissmandel to give his usual Gemara *shiur* in the yeshivah that week. Reb Michel Ber agreed. Before giving the first *shiur*, he opened with a moving introduction, turning to the students and saying with great feeling, "You are fortunate, my dear children, that you have a Rebbe who is like an angel of the Almighty! Anyone who separates himself from him is like one who separates himself from life itself!"

The excellent reputation of Yeshivas She'eiris HaPleitah spread far and wide. One year, several *talmidim* of the yeshivah traveled to Eretz Yisrael to spend the *yamim noraim* with the Belzer Rebbe. The Belzer Rebbe asked them which yeshivah they attended, and they told him that they were students of the Klausenberger Rebbe. The Belzer Rebbe responded with excitement, "*Ah! Torah mit yiras Shamayim tzuvemen!* (Torah and *yiras Shamayim* together!)"

Chapter 3

Taking Action for Klal Yisrael

The Establishment of the Yesodei HaTorah Network

Once the yeshivah's financial situation stabilized somewhat, the Klausenberger looked to expand the scope of the activities of She'eiris HaPleitah. His goal was to eradicate the spiritual devastation that surrounded him. As a first step, he decided to establish a network of religious elementary schools and preschools in the Greater New York region, which he called "Yesodei HaTorah."

The Rebbe's initiative in this endeavor came from the fact that he was concerned not only about his own followers but about all of *klal Yisrael*. "I have seen from experience that it is difficult to save a soul to Torah when the person is an adult, once the atmosphere of materialism and of hedonism have already taken root," he said. "It is imperative to start by educating the children from a very young age. Only that way will it be possible to develop Torah scholars in America."

If it were up to him, he added, he would take the children

under his wing from infancy so that they wouldn't absorb even the slightest trace of negative influence in their parents' homes.

A pioneer in his time, the Klausenberger was the first to establish elementary schools in America that taught in Yiddish and introduced the *alef-beis* in the European style, chanting "*kamatz alef – uh.*" Under the Klausenberger's direction, his *talmidim* and other appointees established elementary schools in Williamsburg, Crown Heights, the Bronx, Brownsville, Boro Park, Kew Gardens, Seagate, and the West Side. These appointees included Rabbis Yechezkel Reich, Yehuda Turner, Shlomo Yehuda Kornfeld, Yehuda Aryeh Hollander, Yeshaya Glick, Meir Schwartz, Leib Ber Pollack, Yitzchak Berger, and Levi Hertz.

The Klausenberger insisted that each principal take personal responsibility for his new institution, starting with its very opening. This often meant going from door to door and convincing the parents to send their children to the *cheder*. The Rebbe, for his part, encouraged the principals and urged them on, even as he placed all administration responsibilities on their shoulders.

The meager income received from the tuition fees was barely enough to cover rent and teachers' salaries. Thus, the remaining funds needed to operate each school had to be raised by the young principals. One of them recalled, "Because I couldn't afford to hire more staff, I had to fill the roles of cook, bus driver, office manager, and substitute teacher myself!"

When one of the young principals complained to the Klausenberger about the job, the Klausenberger responded, "Do you think my position is easier? Would you like to switch places with me?"

"Look at Me"

The Rebbe overlooked everything that went on in the
Yesodei HaTorah schools. On special days like Lag Ba'Omer and
Tu BeShvat, hundreds of children were brought to him for bless-
ings and small presents. The Rebbe would often relate how he
had heard in his childhood a story of the holy *maggid* Rav
Avraham of Trisk. Late in his life, the Maggid once came to
Munkatch, where a large crowd had gathered to hear him speak.
The Maggid told the assembled to lift his chair in the air so that
even the small children would be able to see his face.

Holy men of old would explain the words of Moshe
Rabbeinu, quoted in the *Midrash Rabbah*, "See, I am the one
who has chosen the good," as "Look at me — this is how a Jew
should look."

"So it is with us," said the Klausenberger. "We must be seen
by the young children here in America, so that they will see with
their own eyes what a Jew from the old country looked like."

The Move to the House of Moses Buildings

As the number of students in the Yesodei HaTorah institutions grew, the Klausenberger developed a plan to gather together all the Yesodei HaTorah elementary schools and the yeshivah on a single campus. He purchased several large buildings
for this purpose. The buildings occupied an entire city block on
Stuyvesant Street in Brooklyn and had formerly housed a Jewish
hospital known as the House of Moses.

The Rebbe paid the deposit with a promissory note for
$30,000 that was signed by a wealthy Jew in the oil business. (A

short time later, this man went bankrupt, and it was only through great *siyatta diShmaya* that the debt was paid off.) A long-term mortgage was taken out for the remainder of the purchase price.

Before long, both the yeshivah and the elementary schools were moved into this complex of buildings. The Klausenberger also established a home for children and facilities for the aged and the handicapped on this site.

(After the Rebbe took title to the House of Moses buildings, the buildings were renovated. During the construction, human remains were found in one of the basements. The Rebbe immediately instructed that the remains be buried in a Jewish cemetery after a public funeral held on the seventeenth of Tammuz.)

Years later, when the neighborhood changed and it was necessary to move, the municipality of New York City purchased the buildings for $1 million to make way for a road. A large part of this money was used to pay off the debts which had accumulated over the years from operating the various institutions, and the remaining funds were used to buy the land that ultimately became Kiryat Sanz in Eretz Yisrael.

A Sanctuary and a Diamond

When the yeshivah was ready to move out of its old building and into the House of Moses buildings, the Klausenberger gave a farewell speech based on a *passuk* in that week's parashah, *Parashas Balak*, "How good are your tents, Yaakov, your dwelling place, Israel." The reference to a tent, explained the Rebbe, is to a temporary living space. The word *mishkan*, dwelling place, on the other hand, means a permanent home. The level of Yisrael is a higher level than that of Yaakov. Thus, explained the Klausenberger, one who accepts with love his temporary home, when he is at the level of Yaakov, will ultimately merit a permanent dwelling, when he reaches the level of Yisrael.

The Klausenberger continued his words with the story of his ancestor, Reb Hershele of Ziditchov, the Ateres Tzvi, who for a period of time was extremely poor. Later, he was blessed with an extremely valuable diamond. The saintly Ateres Tzvi wanted no part of the diamond and tried to give it back, saying, "I do not want anything to do with this diamond, except that if one of my offspring shall be in need of it, better that he should find it."

"That diamond," said the Rebbe, "has now found its way to me."

In the same speech, the Klausenberger said, "If I had the means, I would buy an even larger building — even the Empire State Building — because then many parents would be excited to send their children to us and the building would easily fill up with students studying Torah, and a great *kiddush haShem* would result."

In order to transfer the Torah scrolls to the new building, the yeshivah students organized a parade, with singing and dancing in the city streets. The Rebbe donned his *shtreimel* , as did several of his followers, at his request, and joyously in honor of the Torah.

Creating a Summer Camp

In the following years, the Klausenberger opened a summer camp in Woodridge in the Catskills, a summer refuge for the hundreds of children in the Yesodei HaTorah elementary schools which allowed them to spend their summer vacations in a Torah environment in the country.

The Rebbe purchased a hotel facility for the camp at a considerable price. He also encouraged many Williamsburg families to spend the summer there, thus helping to create an atmosphere of Torah and Chassidus in the camp. In later years, the Klausenberger himself went to the camp several times over the course of the summer and spent several restful weeks there.

Bais Chana

Before very long, the Klausenberger also established a religious school for girls in Williamsburg. The school, Bais Chana, opened in 1951 and was named one of the Rebbe's daughters who had perished in the Holocaust. This school was the first chassidic school for girls in the entire United States.

The Rebbe saw an urgent need to establish such an institution for the many children in his community who were approaching school age. To his close associates he explained that although many great rabbis in Hungary and Galicia had opposed the idea of schools for girls, America presented a different reality. In the "new country" it was vital to offer a spiritual refuge for these children.

The Rebbe compared the situation to a dedicated mother who allows her children to play outside without any concern for their health when the weather is pleasant, but on a cold winter day keeps them protected in the warm house or bundled up in warm clothing when they go out. Similarly, the societal influences in Jewish neighborhoods in Europe were not as threatening to impressionable young souls, and thus there was no need to protect the children from the outside world. In America, though, any contact with the outside society was potentially dangerous, and it was imperative to protect the children from it.

As was his wont, the Klausenberger did not approach the establishment of a girls' school half-heartedly. He immersed himself in the project heart and soul, and refused to rely on others for anything connected to the school. Once the school was established, the Rebbe took it upon himself to speak to the students in the older grades several times a year, in order to instill in them the foundations of *emunah*, *ahavas haTorah*, *yiras Shamayim*, *tznius*, and proper character traits, this despite his already overwhelmingly busy schedule. He would speak in the presence of the principal and a number of close associates, while the girls listened closely from an adjoining room.

In later years the Rebbe transferred responsibility for Bais Chana to his oldest daughter, Rebbetzin Miriam Leah. This made it possible for him to be more involved in the educational atmosphere and quality of education in the school.

The Klausenberger believed that it was most important to develop the spiritual character of each student rather than simply educating them with facts and figures, since they were going to be the mothers of the next generation. He was not satisfied with just overseeing the school, and for a certain period of time he would give over to his daughter in-depth *shiurim* on Torah *hashkafah* which she then gave over to the students. After the Rebbe's death, these lectures were published in a book entitled *Derech Chaim*.

The Yesodei HaTorah Congregation

Another important step in the fulfillment of the rebbe's dream of revitalizing Torah life in America was the establishment of Congregation Yesodei HaTorah in Brooklyn, with a community board and a *beis din*. The Rebbe appointed the renowned Rav Yonasan Shteif, *zt"l*, former head of the Budapest *beis din*, as head of the *beis din*. (After Rabbi Shteif passed away, he was replaced by Rav Aharon Yehudah Wilner, *zt"l*.) Other members of the *beis din* included Rav Asher Babad, former head of the *beis din* of Tartkov, Rav Aharon Wieder, former head of the *beis din* of Lindz, and Rav Ephraim Fishel Hershkowitz, former head of the *beis din* of Highlan.

When Rav Shteif was appointed head of the *beis din*, the Rebbe accorded him great respect, as befitting a great Torah scholar of that time. Rabbi Shteif demurred, "Chazal in the *Talmud Yerushalmi* warned that a person who is accorded honor because he is believed to know two chapters when he himself knows that he only knows one is obligated to inform the public that he only knows one chapter properly. And I do not know even a single chapter of the Mishnah!"

To this the Klausenberger responded, "Who can say how much respect should be accorded to a Jew who understands even a single *mishnah*!"

Shiurim for the Public

As the Klausenberger's efforts in child education began to produce results, he turned his attention to adult education and instituted a regular *shiur* for men on Sunday, which for most was not a workday. The Rebbe's goal with this *shiur* was to give the participants a foundation in the basics of Judaism. He concentrated in particular on halachos which even the learned were not aware of. Hundreds of men came each week to study topics such as the laws of tefillin, *yichud*, wigs, immersion in a *mikveh*, lending and borrowing money, the laws of interest, kashrus, slaughtering, and more. These *shiurim*, given in the Rebbe's *beis midrash*, were open to all who wanted to attend.

Even before instituting the Sunday *shiurim*, the Rebbe had begun giving a highly regarded *shiur* in *Pirkei Avos* every Shabbos afternoon. He included in his *shiur* ideas from the entirety of Torah scholarship, which he wove into a beautiful tapestry of Jewish philosophy. He also gave a weekly Thursday night *shiur* in Chumash and *Rashi* which, over the years, drew large audiences.

The Rebbe sternly warned young and old alike to refrain from reading secular newspapers and books. He frequently spoke out publicly against the Conservative and Reform movements and the Zionists, who were a dangerous influence on religious Jews. He also warned of the damage caused by Jewish Communists and Socialists, who secretly attempted to infiltrate yeshivos and synagogues with their destructive propaganda.

One Shavuos afternoon the Klausenberger spoke out emotionally against these evildoers. "Were it in my power, I would call a massive gathering in Madison Square Garden and declare without hesitation, 'Anyone who has a part in Communism has no part in the Jewish people!' "

He recalled a time when he had come to the city of Kashoi, Slovakia, and witnessed a demonstration of "Jews for Communism." The demonstrators were holding red flags in their hands and were led by a Jew "with a beard and *pei'os*, wearing red clothing from head to toe, proclaiming the greatness of Communism."

The Traditions of Our Forefathers

In many of his speeches, the Rebbe would demand of his audiences that they not be satisfied with the minimum observance of Torah and mitzvos, but rather must strive to establish a way of life based on the traditions of Chassidus, with all the *chumros* and *hiddurim* in *tznius, chinuch, kashrus,* and so on, without compromising, even in the slightest way, the traditions and customs of earlier generations.

In one speech, the Rebbe related how the leaders of the Shomer Yisrael organization, an organization of *maskilim* in Galicia, once came to the Belzer Rebbe, Reb Yehoshuale, seemingly to make peace. They said to the Belzer Rebbe, "Why should there be such dissension amongst the Jewish people? Wouldn't it be better if we searched for a common way? We the *maskilim* will respect tradition as best as we can, and on the other side the rabbis and chassidic rebbes will allow certain changes to be instituted in religious life. This way, we will be able to meet in the middle, and the two camps will become closer to one another!"

The saintly Belzer Rebbe listened to their words carefully and asked if he could have a day to consider the matter. The heads of the Shomer Yisrael organization left gleefully, priding themselves in being successful in cracking the wall of the Belzer fortress.

The next day, when they come back for the Rebbe's answer, they were greatly disappointed to hear the Rebbe's words. "All night I considered the matter, wondering what change I could make to the holy customs of the Jewish people which would satisfy you. Suddenly, I had an idea. The purest of Israel have a custom of taking two splinters out of their tables when they cut their nails. Maybe this custom could be done away with and then there would be peace?

"In the end, though, I came to the conclusion that we cannot deviate even one bit from any of the holy customs of the Jewish people, even those that do not have a source in halachah."

It should be remembered that while in later years these ideas were no longer a novelty in America, the Klausenberger accomplished all that he accomplished in the early days after the Holocaust, at a time when areas of religious life like Torah education and kashrus standards were terribly neglected and it was almost impossible to find people who conducted themselves according to the traditional chassidic way of life in the new country.

Caring for the Elderly

The Klausenberger was the first to initiate programs in many other areas, as well. Soon after he arrived in America, he hatched a plan to establish an old age home called *Menuchas Zekeinim* for elderly Jews so that they would be able to spend their later years in a pleasant, Torah-true environment. He appointed Rabbi Nesanel Tzvi Wax to head the enterprise.

Upon this appointment, the Rebbe explained to Reb Nesanel Tzvi that his intention in establishing this institution was to do *chesed* for the living, specifically elderly Jews whose children had abandoned them. He was very pained by the then-common practice of irreligious children putting their elderly parents — even those who had been Torah observant all their lives — into non-Jewish old age homes which included mixed populations of Jews and non-Jews.

The Rebbe went to visit the elderly in Menuchas Zakeinim regularly and blessed them on *erev yom tov* and *erev Yom Kippur.* It was obvious from the faces of these unfortunate Jews, for the most part abandoned by their children, that the Rebbe's visit brought them great joy and happiness.

As was his way, the Rebbe belittled the significance of his actions, and explained regarding the old-age home, "When I first saw the suffering of the elderly in America, I wanted to help them with all my heart, but I knew that even if I were to build a ten-story building for them it would not be big enough... I therefore concentrated on establishing a yeshivah and elementary schools that would educate the next generation to honor and respect their parents. Once this education yielded results, I knew there would not be the same need to care for the elderly, since their children would be able to take care of them.

"Now that this has been accomplished, I am able to establish this one small home, which is not that overwhelming of a proposition."

A Leader Among Leaders

The Kopishnitzer Rebbe, Reb Avraham Yehoshua Heshel, was seated next to the Rebbe at the opening ceremony of Menuchas Zekeinim. In the midst of the ceremony, a man approached the Klausenberger with a question regarding surgery for a sick person. The Klausenberger turned to the Kopishnitzer Rebbe and asked his opinion, noting that the man who posed the question was well known to him.

The Kopishnitzer Rebbe replied, "I don't know enough to answer this question. Whenever I am asked such a question I beseech the Almighty that, in the merit of my holy ancestors, He endow me with the wisdom and understanding necessary to answer it properly. But if I wasn't the one asked, how can I possibly respond? Better that you decide the matter yourself, since you are the one who was asked."

(It should be noted that the Kopishnitzer Rebbe was one of the Klausenberger's greatest admirers. He stood by the Rebbe during trying times and raised desperately needed funds for the She'eiris HaPleitah institutions. At every opportunity he publicized the importance of the Klausenberger's efforts to spread *Yiddishkeit* in America, and he also prayed regularly for the Rebbe's health and well-being, since he believed that the Jewish world at the time was in dire need of the Rebbe's leadership.)

Raising Kashrus Standards

At every opportunity, the Klausenberger worked to improve the religious standards of American Jewry. To this end, he often convened meetings with other *rabbanim* to discuss and develop new plans for improving spiritual life in America.

In addition, the Rebbe raised awareness of many areas of Jewish religious life that were being neglected in America. At times he spoke out about the deficient kashrus standards and practices then in existence in the slaughter of poultry and the handling of meat and insisted that certain halachic stringencies in matzah baking that had been followed in Europe be reestablished. He also protested against the widespread sale of defective mezuzos and tefillin and spoke out against the practice of not burying the deceased in a timely fashion. When *esrogim* were imported from Morocco for use on Sukkos, the Rebbe announced that only *esrogim* that had the proper qualities and were from orchards with a long-standing tradition of acceptability could be used.

The Rebbe once met Rav Levi Yitzchak Greenwald of Tzehlem at a *sheva berachos*. In the course of the meal, the Klausenberger asked him, "I heard the *rav* has given a *hechsher* to an oil factory. Was the *rav* present at the factory when the nuts were crushed?" Reb Levi Yitzchak assured him that in the future he would make certain to be present even when the nuts were being crushed.

On another occasion, Rav Greenwald issued a halachic ruling permitting the lowering of the flame on a gas range on *yom tov*. When the Klausenberger learned of this ruling, he visited Rabbi Greenwald at his home to discuss the issue in detail. After much halachic discussion, Reb Levi Yitzchak concurred with the Rebbe's viewpoint and issued a public statement retracting his ruling.

The Klausenberger also strongly encouraged the leaders of Arugos HaBosem community of Tzehlem to build a community *mikveh* in Williamsburg with all the halachic requirements and embellishments. Reb Levi Yitzchak endorsed the Klausenberger's request and the Tzehlem community undertook responsibility for the project. This *mikveh* was the first *mikveh* in Williamsburg built according to the halachic standards of the Divrei Chaim. The Rebbe made a considerable contribution to the project, and when its construction was complete he was invited to inspect it personally and offer his certification.

Kollel

The Klausenberger had original ideas on every subject and aspect of Jewish life, ideas which were conceived and developed out of his deep desire to sanctify Hashem's name. He would constantly recall the words of Rabbeinu Yonah of Gerondi in *Shaarei Teshuvah*, "One of the ways of sanctifying Hashem's name is to demonstrate with every expression of the lips, every suggestion of the eyes, and every movement of the body that the foundation of man's soul and his goodness, purpose, and essence is the service of Hashem, fearing Him and His Torah. This is the essence of man."

The Klausenberger was therefore among the very first to establish a *kollel* for young married men in the new country. Immediately upon his arrival in America he realized that, because of the deplorable state of religious life in the country, it was vital to encourage young men to continue learning after their marriage, despite the fact that this had not been common practice in Europe.

If there was no institution of full-time Torah learning in America, he felt, the glory of Torah would be entirely forgotten in the new country. In addition, there was a real threat to a young man's *frumkeit* if he went out to the workplace immediately after marriage. The Rebbe spoke often about this in impassioned public speeches which he gave in Brownsville, the East

Side, the Bronx, Boro Park, Queens, Flatbush, and Crown Heights, to audiences that included all types of Jews.

The *kollel* founded by the Rebbe, known as Kollel Avreichim Ohel Moshe, in memory of one of the Rebbe's sons who had perished in the Holocaust, was the first chassidic *kollel* in America. At one point, the Rebbe tried to organize a group of Torah scholars from the *kollel* to collect the sayings of every *tanna* and *amora* mentioned in the Talmud into a separate book so that one could study each Sage's thought process and approach and thereby understand his thinking. On a different occasion, the Rebbe instructed *kollel* members to research certain complex laws of divorce and a *sefer* of their insights on the topic was then prepared for publication.

A Tenth Man for the Minyan

The Rebbe once instructed Rabbi Michel Weiss and Rabbi Nesanel Tzvi Wax, the principals of the *talmud Torah* in Crown Heights, to organize a minyan in the school on Shabbos in order to strengthen and uplift the school. The two young men dissented, respectfully explaining that the majority of the parents lived too far away from the school and would not come in to daven. But the Rebbe was insistent.

Rabbi Weiss recalled, "On the first Shabbos we waited in vain to begin. The sun was already at its height and only nine people had come: we were short one for a minyan. Reb Nesanel Tzvi and I went out to search for a tenth man. Finally, we found someone who agreed to join us, but we weren't sure if he was Jewish or not because he sat like a *golem* the entire *tefillah*!"

A similar incident happened to the Rebbe himself at around

the same time, one Friday evening after nightfall. His students brought in a passersby to complete the minyan. The man had a beard and *pei'os* and was dressed in the traditional garb of a religious Jew. As they began to daven, however, the thought crossed the Rebbe's mind: *Perhaps this man is not really Jewish?*

After the *tefillah* was over, the Rebbe turned to one of the young boys who had brought the man in from the street and asked him who the man was. After some investigation it was discovered that the man was a convert.

After Shabbos, the Rebbe sent for him and inquired, "Who converted you? Where did the conversion take place?" and other questions of this nature. The man responded that he had been converted by a rabbi in Montreal and a doctor in the local hospital had performed his circumcision. Afterwards, he had been given keys to a swimming pool, where he performed his immersion in private.

Because it had to be established completely that the man had not properly been converted and was thus still a non-Jew, the Rebbe telephoned the "rabbi" in Montreal and asked him about this so called "conversion." The rabbi offered various excuses but did not give the Rebbe a direct answer. However, the Klausenberger made a point of meeting with this rabbi face to face and asked him: "How did you do such a thing?!"

The rabbi stammered a bit and finally admitted that it was really his wife who had handled the conversion and that as a matter of principle he did not get involved in his wife's activities!

An Obligation to Rebuke

The Rebbe once noted, "We find with respect to Noach that

the Torah describes him as *tamim b'dorosav* — pure in his generations.' Some of the Sages interpret this description as a criticism of Noach; had he lived in the generation of Avraham, he would not have been highly regarded. The reasoning behind this criticism is that Avraham rebuked the people who lived in his times and was therefore despised by them. Noach, on the other hand, did not rebuke his fellowman and was therefore respected by them. As our Sages explain, 'A rabbi for whom the residents of the city have compassion — it is not because he is admired but, rather, because he does not rebuke them.

"The Torah hints, therefore, that had Noach lived in the time of Avraham and learned from him not to be reluctant to rebuke his fellowman, surely then he would not have been respected at all, and they would have belittled him, too."

Chapter 4

Expanding Horizons

A Yeshivah in Montreal

In 1948 a group of young *bachurim* who could not obtain entry visas into the United States arrived in Montreal, Canada. The *bachurim* had been students in the Rebbe's yeshivah in Germany, and the Rebbe, concerned for their spiritual welfare, immediately sent Rabbi Menashe Klein to Montreal to establish a yeshivah for them there. The Rebbe also traveled to Montreal to see them personally, accompanied by Rabbi Yosef Binyamin Williger, who was assigned the task of renting facilities for a dormitory and setting up a dining room for the newly established yeshivah.

As soon as the yeshivah was officially opened, the Klausenberger sent a group of *bachurim* from Williamsburg to learn there for a while and strengthen the new establishment. Rav Pinchas Hirschpring (a grandson of the Gaon from Dukla, Rav Tevele Zahman, *zt"l*), who immigrated to Montreal after the war and later became the city's chief rabbi, also helped the Klausenberger in this effort.

A Future for the Jewish People

The story is told that when the Rebbe traveled to Montreal, he met with the head of the local Jewish Federation, a Mr. Nemerov, and asked for his financial assistance in the establishment of the new yeshivah.

Nemerov, who was one of the wealthiest Jews in Montreal, asked the Rebbe, "Why do we need a yeshivah? We already have a Jewish school in this city!"

The Rebbe responded with a question, "How many children attend your school?"

"Several hundred," answered Nemerov quickly.

"And how many of them do you think will remain Jewish?" asked the Rebbe.

"Hopefully twenty percent," answered Mr. Nemerov.

"That means approximately sixty children..." the Rebbe said thoughtfully. "Let's think of the long term for a moment. When each of these children marries and has a family, how many children do you think they'll have on average?"

"Probably two children," answered the man.

The Rebbe continued to press his point, "And from that generation of children, how many will remain Orthodox Jews?"

"About twenty percent," came the response.

"This means," the Rebbe said, "that according to your estimate, in forty years, from this Jewish day school, there will be eighty-five religious Jews. In my yeshivah, however, which today numbers thirty students, please G-d, one hundred percent will remain religious Jews. The average family of each student will be ten children. In the next generation, one hundred percent will also remain religious Jews, and they too will be blessed with

families of ten children on average. Thus, in forty years we will
have three thousand Orthodox Jews from our school versus
eighty-five from your school. Now tell me, from whom will the
Jewish people be built and sustained? From your school or from
ours?"

Convinced by the Rebbe's arguments, the man pledged a
large sum of money to the yeshivah, which was named Mesivta
Reishis Chochmah, like its counterpart in Williamsburg.

Appointing a Rosh Yeshivah

The Rebbe would often explain the incident of Rabbi Yosei
ben Kisma in the following manner: As related in *Pirkei Avos*, the
great Sage was offered thousands of gold coins to come and live
in a particular city. He refused, saying, "Even if you were to give
me all the gold, silver, and jewels in the world I would only live
in a place of Torah" (*Avos* 6:11).

How did Rabbi Yosei ben Kisma know that the place he was
being asked to move to was not a place of Torah? The answer, explained the Rebbe, is that this great Sage, knowing the low spiritual level of the Jewish people at that time, asked himself, "Why
do they have this tremendous desire to give a Torah scholar
thousands of gold coins and jewels? This must be the work of
the *yetzer hara*, who wants to trick me into leaving a city of Torah
study and moving to a place of *amei ha'aretz*."

The Klausenberger no doubt had this story in mind when
he offered the position of *rosh hayeshivah* of Mesivta Reishis
Chochmah of Montreal to Rav Shmuel Unsdorfer, who was living in England at the time. With the invitation, he issued a warning: it would not be an easy task. "The moment that building the

yeshivah becomes easy for you," the Rebbe told Rav Unsdorfer, "a thorough investigation is called for, lest it is the success of the *sitra achra, chas v'shalom.*"

Rav Unsdorfer, however, was not deterred, and took the position. Under his leadership and dedication, Montreal eventually became a vibrant Torah center. The presence of the yeshivah spurred the development of other educational institutions and of the Reishis Chochmah Congregation. In addition, the Klausenberger visited Montreal several times a year and was a great spiritual influence on the Jews of the city. His words to Rav Shmuel Unsdorfer, "I am confident that in the merit of my holy ancestors, any place that I travel to for the purpose of bringing honor to Hashem and His Torah will eventually become a place of Torah," were indeed fulfilled.

Rav Shmuel Unsdorfer (who later became the Rebbe's *mechutan* when his daughter married the Rebbe's son) lived to see his legacy continue on, as his sons lead communities and Torah institutions the world over. Rav Unsdorfer later moved to Eretz Yisrael and became the *rav* of Congregation Divrei Chaim of Sanz in Petach Tikvah.

A Yeshivah in Mexico

In 1952 the Klausenberger made a revolutionary move when he founded Yeshivas Reishis Chochmah in Mexico City, for children of Sephardic families who had emigrated there from Syria. He appointed Rav Shmuel Krasna, an American-born *talmid chacham* who was a student of Mesivta Torah Vodaas, to head the school.

The idea of opening a yeshivah in Mexico, which was a spiritual desert at the time, seemed like an impossible dream. But with the Rebbe's support and encouragement, Rabbi Krasna turned this dream into a reality. Reb Shmuel studied to be a *shochet* so that he could fill this need, too, while his wife started a *frum* school for girls, with the Rebbe's approval, and brought many individuals back to Judaism. During the years that the Krasnas lived in Mexico, approximately seven hundred boys and girls studied in the two institutions.

Shortly after the yeshivah opened, the Rebbe decided to visit Mexico personally to see the activities that were going on there and to evaluate the community's needs. There was great anticipation in the Mexican Jewish community as Rebbe's arrival approached. A royal welcome was arranged for him, and hundreds of people, Ashkenazic and Sephardic alike, gathered in the street to greet him and get a glimpse of his holy face. Even non-Jews gathered to watch the spectacular scene.

The Rebbe stayed in Mexico for a week. Much of his time there was spent encouraging and supporting the community leaders, showing them great love and admiration and exhorting them not to spare any effort on behalf of Torah, especially with regard to the children. In addition, the Rebbe's intensity and *avodas Hashem* were an amazing inspiration for the local Jewish population, who had never seen anything like it before. Saul Zeis, who drove the Klausenberger to the *mikveh* twice a day during his visit, said that the vision of the Rebbe pouring his heart out during *tefillah* and singing *zemiros* on Friday night would never leave him.

One evening the Klausenberger davened *maariv* in the beautiful Sephardic synagogue in Mexico City, which was filled to capacity in honor of the occasion. Both men and women wiped away tears as they listened to the Rebbe pleading with his Father in Heaven like a small child. At the conclusion of the *tefillah*, the Rebbe walked to the *bimah*, turned around to face the crowd, and cried out, with great emotion, "*Barcheinu, Avinu, kulanu k'echad yachad b'or panecha. Kulanu achim yehudim, b'nei Keil chai* — Bless us, our Father, all of us as one with the light of Your face. We are all brothers, Jews, children of the living G-d!"

He then stepped down from the *bimah* without another word. Yet the sweetness and purity with which he uttered those few words remained with all those assembled for a long time afterwards. They all experienced, at that moment, a tangible expression of the Rebbe's fierce love for every single Jew, descendant of Avraham, Yitzchak, and Yaakov, however far from Yiddishkeit he might be.

With undescribable desire and longing, the crowd surged to the front of the sanctuary to be greeted by the Rebbe, who looked at each one with great warmth and love, as if he was his brother.

Upon the Rebbe's return from Mexico, he changed the *nusach* of the *Shabbos Mevarchim* blessing slightly, adding in the last paragraph, after the words, "*Yechadesheihu HaKadosh Baruch Hu aleinu v'al kol amo beis Yisrael* — may Hashem renew it upon us and upon all of Israel," the phrase, "*b'chol makom sheheim* — wherever they may be."

The Publication of Yisrael Saba

As the branches of the She'eris HaPleitah yeshivos in America and Canada began to grow, the Klausenberger gave his stamp of approval to the decision to publish a monthly journal, *Yisrael Saba*, which would include aggadic and halachic dissertations of both teachers and students alike. In a congratulatory letter issued on the occasion of the publication of the journal's first issue, the Klausenberger wrote, "I was pleased by the administration's idea of publishing a journal which will inspire students to develop original Torah insights and sharpen their minds, each according to his own ability, in the ways of our holy ancestors...and prevent them from following the emptiness of secular wisdoms...and encourage them to understand the glory, honor, and beauty of the words of Torah, which are more desirable than gold."

Rabbi Avraham Weinfeld, an alumnus of the yeshivah, was appointed the first editor of *Yisrael Saba*, which published a number of the Rebbe's lectures and insights, as well as lectures given by the *rosh yeshivah* Rav Wilner, in addition to insights of the rebbeim in the yeshivah and *chiddushim* of the *yeshivah bachurim* and *kollel* members. The journal also included discourses on important practical issues of interest to the Orthodox community.

The first edition of *Yisrael Saba* was published in Adar 1953. After a short while, publication stopped, but then was resumed in Eretz Yisrael, where it was published continuously for many years.

A Unique Approach to Kvittlach

From the day that the Klausenberger first settled in Williamsburg, Jews of all walks of life came to seek his blessing and ask his advice, bringing their requests written on *kvittlach*, accompanied by donations for the Rebbe. The Rebbe, however, had an unusual practice. Rather than keeping the donations for himself, he would fill out a receipt for the contribution from one of the She'eiris HaPleitah institutions.

When a close friend of the Klausenberger asked him about this, the Klausenberger responded humbly and simply, "My father, of blessed memory, was a tzaddik. When he was presented with a *kvittel*, he would pray for the individual until the Almighty answered his prayers and assisted the person. I am not on the same level as my father. I do not have the power to do anything. I can only take the money for the yeshivah and ask Hashem to send a salvation to the person in need in the merit of the *tzedakah* that he has given to the yeshivah.

"My family knows nothing of this, and they might think that the money is mine and they can use it. I don't want to steal from them, so I write out a receipt for every contribution. I also want the person who brought the money to know that it is not mine, as it says, 'And you shall be pure before Hashem and Israel.' "

One time a man brought the Rebbe a *kvittel* accompanied by fifteen dollars. However, before the Rebbe could give him a receipt, he left the room quickly. Even though it was wintertime and there was snow on the ground outside, the Rebbe rose and ran after him. After an exhausting chase in the streets of Williamsburg, the Rebbe finally caught up with the man and gave him the receipt. Only then was his mind at ease.

A Rebbe to All in Need

The chassidim who were close to the Klausenberger knew that they could turn to him at any time of day or night. One time the wife of a certain chassid was in labor. The doctors said that she was in grave danger and they needed to operate. The distraught chassid called the Klausenberger at two in the morning to ask him to pray for his wife. The Rebbe instructed him to immediately immerse himself in a *mikveh*, and his wife's condition would improve.

The chassid left the hospital to follow these instructions, but it took him a while to find a *mikveh* that was open at that hour of the night. Finally immersing himself, he returned to the hospital, where he was informed that his wife had given birth and all was well.

The Rebbe's Personal Avodah

Despite the Klausenberger's increasing obligations towards the public, his own daily regimen remained the same. Reb Avraham Eideles, who served as the Rebbe's *shamash* for two years, beginning in the summer of 1949, related that during the weekdays the Klausenberger never lay down to sleep at all, and when he allowed himself a few moments of slumber, he only removed his socks and shoes for this purpose. The Klausenberger once dozed off sitting by his Gemara in the middle of the day. He woke up immediately and called Reb Avraham, who was in the yeshivah building, to please bring him *negel vasser*, because even during the day he didn't want to get up without first washing his hands.

"The boundaries between day and night did not exist in the Rebbe's world," recalled Reb Avraham. "During *Selichos*, for example, the Rebbe would end his *shalosh seudos tisch* at four in the morning, and a short time later would be getting up to recite *Selichos*. On Hoshana Rabbah, he would finish reciting *hoshanos* late in the afternoon, close to the start of Shemini Atzeres, and would quickly go into the sukkah to eat something and say *divrei Torah* on topics relating to Hoshana Rabbah, even though there was no one in the sukkah with him."

Reb Avraham also recalled that when the Klausenberger sat down to eat on the first night of Sukkos, he would first take a small portion of challah to fulfill the mitzvah of eating in the sukkah and then take a second portion to fulfill the obligation of eating a meal on *yom tov*. His *chassidim* would say in jest that the food the Klausenberger consumed on Sukkos gave him strength for the entire year!

The Rebbe's Tefillos

Great numbers of chassidim streamed to the Klausenberger's *beis midrash* to listen to his fiery *tefillos*. When the Rebbe davened, he was an awesome sight to behold, the likes of which had not been witnessed in many generations. The words spilled from his mouth like fiery embers, and he would recite them with tears streaming from his eyes, with such intensity that he seemed consumed by fire.

The Rebbe could repeat a verse or a paragraph ten times, each time with a different intonation. When he reached the verse in *Az Yashir*, "*Tevi'eimo v'sita'eimo b'har nachalasecha,* You shall bring them and implant them on the mountain of Your heritage," he would plead with the Almighty for the redemption of the Jewish people, sobbing, "*Tatte, Tatte, Tatte...oy, oy, oy... Tatte,* have mercy on Your children... *Tevi'eimo...v'sita'eimo... Tatte,* Tatte, Tatte, it is enough already, enough, have mercy on your children... *Heileger Bashefer,* bring them now, now...implant them on the mountain of Your heritage..." At times it would take him close to an hour to recite these words alone.

It is difficult to adequately describe the awe-inspiring scene of the Rebbe reciting the phrase in *Birchos Kerias Shema,* "*Avinu Ha'Av HaRachaman, HaMerachem racheim aleinu* — Our Father, the merciful Father, Who acts mercifully, have mercy upon us." A torrent of tears would pour from his eyes as he begged again and again, "Instill in our hearts wisdom to understand and elucidate...to listen...to learn and to teach...to safeguard, perform, and fulfill all the words of Your Torah's teaching with love."

Without additional understanding and enlightenment in Torah, he felt that life was simply not worth living. He would sob like a man begging desperately for his life, "My Father, my merciful Father, the Merciful One, have mercy on me and give me life! Instill in my heart understanding so that I may understand and elucidate the words of Your Torah! Instill in my heart the desire and will to safeguard, perform, and fulfill all the words of Your Torah with love!"

The Rebbe's Tisches

The *tisches* that the Klausenberger held on Shabbos and on *yom tov* also left an indelible impression on all who were present there. Some were inspired by the emotional singing. Others were moved by the Rebbe's *divrei Torah* and his deep insights into the word of Hashem. One of the chassidim recalled, "One Shabbos when I was just fourteen, I was standing behind the Rebbe's chair at *shalosh seudos*. The Rebbe was speaking with great emotion as he delivered words of inspiration for the days of the *Shovevim*. Suddenly, a thought crossed my mind: *If the spiritual impact of an aveirah is so great on the neshamah, why is it never mentioned in the Torah?*

"At that very moment the Rebbe turned and looked behind his chair, directly to the place where I was standing, and cried out, 'This sin is so severe and its impact is so terrible that it does not even need to be written down!'

"I was stunned. It was as if the Rebbe had read my mind."

"We Are All One Nation"

The Rebbe's concern for *klal Yisrael* extended far beyond the needs of his own community. At a conference that was once held of all the great *rabbanim* and *roshei yeshivah* of the time, the Klausenberger suggested a practical plan to help the *frum* community in Eretz Yisrael, which was then suffering at the hands of the secular Israeli government. The Rebbe made his plan conditional on the total involvement of all those present.

One *rav* present asked, "We are two different worlds, Chassidish and Litvish. How will we be able to work together?"

The Klausenberger answered, "There are forty-nine separate states in this country, and each one has its own laws and government. What is permitted in one state is forbidden in another. Nevertheless, these states have found common ground between them, a single language and a single purpose, and are joined together in a union which has produced the greatest country in the world. Now, I ask you, because we say '*veyitzmach pirkunai*' in Kaddish and you do not, is that a reason why we cannot join forces together? We are all the children of the same Father, our Father in Heaven, and we are all His children."

Hearing the Rebbe's answer, the *rav* had nothing more to say.

The Klausenberger always used to say, "Some recite *Hodu* before *Baruch She'amar* and some recite *Baruch She'amar* before *Hodu*. But all bow down at '*Yehi chevod Hashem le'olam,*' i.e., when it comes to *kevod Shamayim*."

The Rebbe also used to quote the verse, "There is abundant peace for the lovers of Torah and there is no stumbling block for them" (*Tehillim* 119:65) and explain: "No obstacle can interfere with the great peace that will dwell among those who love Your Torah." Or in other words, the *yetzer hara*, who is called an obstacle by the Prophet Yeshayah, will disintegrate when the lovers of Torah desire to live together in peace.

With Other Torah Giants of the Generation

During the years that the Klausenberger lived in America, he forged a close friendship with many other Torah giants of the time. When the Rebbe's son, Reb Tzvi Elimelech, was born, the bris was attended by many great *rabbanim*, including Rav Moshe Feinstein, *zt"l*, who made special efforts to join in the *simchah*. The *mohel* was Rav Liepele Teitelbaum, *zt"l*, the Sassover Rebbe, and the *sandek* was the Strapkover Rebbe, Rabbi Menachem Mendel Halberstam, *zt"l*. The baby was named Tzvi Elimelech after the Klausenberger's grandfather, the B'nei Yissaschar of Dinov.

When the Rebbe's second son was born, the *sandek* was the Boyaner Rebbe, Reb Mordechai Shlomo, *zt"l*, and the *mohel* was the Tzehlemer Rav, Rav Levi Yitzchak Greenwald, while the Seret-Vizhnitzer Rebbe, Reb Baruchel, *zt"l*, was honored with the recitation of the blessings. The newborn was named Shmuel Dovid after the Rebbe's father-in-law, the Gaon of Nitra, author of the *Neos Desheh*.

A Visit with Rav Henkin

The Klausenberger once went to pay a visit to the great *gaon* Rabbi Yosef Eliyahu Henkin, *zt"l*, a famous Torah scholar and a leading halachic authority of the time. Rav Henkin welcomed the Rebbe with great respect and friendship, and they had an enjoyable Torah discussion together. Suddenly the telephone in Rav Henkin's study rang. The caller asked Rav Henkin for his opinion on a very important and serious matter of halachah. Out of respect for the Klausenberger, Rav Henkin did not rule on the matter immediately and asked the caller to call back in ten minutes.

After he had hung up, Rav Henkin presented the question to the Rebbe and asked him for his opinion. The Rebbe, however, responded that he was unable to answer such a difficult question without first giving it careful thought.

When the Rebbe left Rav Henkin, he sent one of the *talmidim* to borrow certain *sefarim* for him. Then, secluding himself in his study for several hours, he researched the matter thoroughly and wrote a lengthy responsa on the question, detailing all the halachic opinions on the matter and analyzing them with his usual clarity of thought. He sent the responsa by messenger to Rav Henkin, who agreed with the Rebbe's ruling and was amazed at his ability to write such a detailed, well-organized and thought-out responsa in such a short period of time.

"Truthfully," Rav Henkin said, "I did not need to read through the entire discussion which he sent me — it would have been sufficient for me to simply look at his conclusion, but the Rebbe's Torah discussions are beloved to me."

A Visit to Telz

On another occasion the Rebbe happened to visit the Telz Yeshivah in Cleveland, a yeshivah headed by the renowned Torah scholars Rav Elya Meir Bloch and Rav Chaim Mordechai Katz. The two *roshei yeshivah* gave the Rebbe a royal welcome and asked him to give the student body a *shiur* in halachah. The Rebbe asked what topic the *shiur* should be on, and he was told, "It would be good if you based your *shiur* on the *sugya* which the yeshivah is currently studying, *Maseches Kiddushin daf gimmel.*"

"Fine," said the Rebbe. He turned and ascended the *bimah* in the yeshivah's *beis midrash*, faced the hundreds of attentive students, and without any preparation at all proceeded to give a complicated lecture which astounded his audience. For over an hour the Klausenberger discussed all the opinions of the *rishonim* on the *sugya*. Then he raised many issues and resolved each question with piercing analysis as if he was in the midst of learning the *sugya* himself.

The *shiur* remained a topic of discussion among the *yeshivah bachurim* for a long time afterwards.

A Spiritual Center

Several years after the Klausenberger arrived in Williamsburg, Rav Baruch Frankel, a philanthropist and close confidant of the Rebbe, mentioned to him that he was seriously considering the purchase of a building in the heart of Williamsburg, on Lee Avenue. It seemed to him that it would be the perfect location for a large supermarket.

"Would it not be perfect for a *beis midrash?*" responded the Rebbe.

Reb Baruch understood the hint and immediately consented to the Rebbe's request. He purchased the building with his own funds and renovated it for use as the Sanz-Klausenberger *beis midrash*. The Rebbe never forgot Reb Baruch's generosity and named the building "Beis Baruch" in Reb Baruch's honor (the name it carries to this day).

Over the years this building became the spiritual center for thousands of chassidim in Williamsburg and other places. Masses of Jews streamed to the *beis midrash*, beginning with the Holocaust survivors whose initial contact with the Rebbe had been in the DP camps in Germany — but not ending there. Many more people came, people who were attracted by the Rebbe's fiery prayers, his intense *derashos*, and his *tisches*, which he conducted for hundreds of followers.

The numbers of chassidim who turned to the Rebbe for guidance and inspiration and love grew from year to year, as Sanz-Klausenberg communities sprang up in Williamsburg, Boro Park, Monsey, Montreal, and many other locations. In later years the Rebbe also turned to New Jersey, where he established the beautiful chassidic community of Union City. From 1973 to

1986, the Rebbe himself lived in Union City, where he built a yeshivah and other educational institutions.

It should be noted that it was not only the Sanz-Klausenberg community that benefitted from the Rebbe's spiritual influence. Rather, as a result of the spiritual awakening that he engendered in the American Jewish community, many other Torah organizations and institutions were established. The Rebbe was truly a significant factor in the spiritual revolution that occurred in his time in American Jewry.

Chapter 5

Longing for Zion

A Promise to Move to Eretz Yisrael

Although the Klausenberger spent fifteen years in America, his yearning for Eretz Yisrael never ceased, and he remained steadfast to the promise he had made to himself during the Holocaust, in the midst of his suffering, that if he merited to survive the Nazi hell he would move to Eretz Yisrael. When he left Germany he said, "I am traveling to Eretz Yisrael by way of America."

Rav Yechezkel Besser, a Radomsker chassid, once asked the Rebbe for his source of his deep love for Eretz Yisrael. In response, the Rebbe opened his desk drawer and removed a small book entitled *Kollel HaIvrim — Machazir Atarah L'Yoshnah*, written by Rabbi Akiva Yosef Schlesinger. "This book and its author have had a profound influence on me," he explained. "Its words connected my soul to Eretz Yisrael and made me long to live there. If only the author's words had been heeded years ago, when the book was first published, the picture of the Jewish world today would be completely different..."

The Rebbe then added, "If our brothers had followed Reb

Akiva Yosef's suggestion, it is very likely that hundreds of thousands of Jews — even millions — would have been saved from annihilation in the Holocaust, and our Holy Land would look completely different today. To our great despair, though, the Satan and his cohorts succeeded in preventing this."

"No One Longs for Eretz Yisrael As I Do"

The Klausenberger was completely devoted to Eretz Yisrael, and he was always interested in what was happening there. On Tishah B'Av of 1946, Rabbi Menachem Porush, one of the greatest activists of the *frum* world at the time, was staying with the Rebbe. After reciting *Kinnos* at night, the Rebbe called Rabbi Porush in to his room and questioned him at length on what was happening in Eretz Yisrael. This scene repeated itself on the following day after *Kinnos* were recited as well.

Reb Yisrael Shimon Kastelanitz, a well-known scribe from Eretz Yisrael, visited the Klausenberger in 1953 and asked him why he did not come to visit Eretz Yisrael. The Rebbe answered, "No one longs for the Holy Land more than I do. But once I come there, I will not be able to leave again, and the time has not yet come for me to leave what I am doing here."

The year before, a similar incident occurred when the Vizhnitzer Rebbe, Rabbi Chaim Meir, *zt"l*, the Imrei Chaim, came to America. Words cannot adequately describe the affection he and the Klausenberger had for each other when they met. When they parted, the Klausenberger said, "If only you could take me back to Eretz Yisrael in your suitcase!" The Vizhnitzer Rebbe responded, "They would charge too large of a duty for such a valuable package!"

The Rebbe's First Institutions in the Holy Land

By 1948 the Klausenberger had already established his committee for the She'eiris HaPleitah in Eretz Yisrael. He assigned this organization the task of welcoming the new immigrants that were streaming into the Holy Land and establishing schools and other religious centers to absorb them. The immigrants, who came largely from the frum communities of Hungary and Romania and arrived in Eretz Yisrael with little more than the clothes on their backs, were ambushed by secularists from every direction, and the Rebbe spread his protective net over them from afar in an effort to keep their children on the religious path.

For reasons known only to himself, the Klausenberger focused his attention on the city of Tzefas, where his emissaries, Reb Yechezkel Neuwirth and Reb Shimon Diamond, established a She'eiris HaPleitah elementary school for boys. Close to one hundred children studied in the school, which was the only one of its kind in the entire Upper Galilee. A parallel Bais Yaakov school for girls and a preschool were also established under the Rebbe's guidance. A She'eiris HaPleitah *beis midrash* and Torah center followed, led by the *gaon* Rav Zev Wolf Ternover, formerly the *rav* of the Romanian town of Shatz.

Each of these institutions was supported faithfully by the Klausenberger, who expended significant efforts in raising the funds necessary for their survival. The same actions were repeated in many other cities: Be'er Sheva, Azor, Kfar Nitzachon, and more. Wherever new religious immigrants had settled, the Rebbe sent his emissaries to establish schools for both boys and girls under the auspices of She'eiris HaPleitah. These schools were the spiritual salvation of generations of Jews.

The institutions were run strictly in accordance with Torah law. The spoken language was Yiddish, and the curricula were faithful to the traditions of earlier generations. The number of religious Jews that these institutions saved is unimaginable.

Efforts for Bais Yaakov HaYashan

The Klausenberger was also extremely devoted to the Bais Yaakov HaYashan in Yerushalayim, which had been established in 1921 under the leadership of the *gaon* Rabbi Yosef Chaim Sonnenfeld and the *maggid* Rabbi Bentzion Yadler. Lacking funds and adequate facilities, the school met with hard times and almost closed its doors. Hearing of the dire straits that the institution found itself in, the Klausenberger pledged to take it under his wings and save it from closing. He was responsible for the school's rebirth and expansion to an enrollment of six hundred girls, from preschool age through seminary, including a vocational school and teacher-training courses.

The Klausenberger also encouraged the school's administration to open new branches in other Jerusalem neighborhoods, such as Shaarei Chesed and Batei Broide, to serve the poverty-stricken families living there. The Rebbe's vision also inspired the establishment of Bnos Rochel, an organization that provided girls who had completed their formal education with a proper social and religious framework until their marriage.

From his home in Williamsburg, the Rebbe wrote the following words to the school administrators in Yerushalayim: "I am very pleased that your work is succeeding, with Hashem's help, in increasing the glory of Torah and in raising pure Jewish mothers committed to the spirit of Torah in the ways of our tradition and the paths of our ancestors. May Hashem Yisbarach assist us all, in the merit of our holy ancestors, to succeed in strengthening the weak and in bringing *Yiddishe neshamos* closer to their pure source, so that they bring *nachas* to their Father in Heaven."

Rebuilding the City of Yavneh

Parallel to the Klausenberger's efforts to develop Torah institutions for young children, the Rebbe also sought to open a yeshivah that would produce *talmidei chachamim* and halachic authorities like the yeshivah that he had in Klausenberg before the war. The Rebbe assigned his student Rav Yisrael Aryeh Zalmanovitz, author of the *sefer Chayei Nefesh*, to this task.

The Rebbe also appointed Rav Zalmanovitz as the *rav* of the ancient city of Yavneh, near Nachal Sorek, where a large community of religious Jews from Transylvania had settled. In this location, the Rebbe envisioned a rebirth of the Yavneh of old, which had been a refuge and a Torah center in Talmudic times. Here he wanted to rebuild the Torah world of Hungary that had been destroyed by the Nazis.

These were the first seeds of the enormous field of Torah that would develop under the Rebbe's guidance in the years to come, as Sanz yeshivos, Kollel HaShas branches, and Mifal HaShas institutions began to flourish throughout Eretz Yisrael and the Diaspora.

The following letter, one of the many that the Klausenberger wrote during this period to Rav Zalmanovitz about the yeshivah, sheds light on this link in the chain of awesome activities that the

Klausenberger undertook to spread Torah throughout the world, and particularly in Eretz Yisrael.

> *My dear friend and student, the great rav whose Torah knowledge and yiras Shamayim are outstanding, the distinguished halachic authority, Yisrael Aryeh, shlita,*
>
> *After inquiring of your welfare, I write to assist you, with Hashem's help, in establishing a yeshivah for young men who are diligent students of the Torah in the ways of old. I look forward to the day when you will be learning with them, spreading Torah and yiras Shamayim, and I will help you in any way I can, with Hashem's help. I would like the yeshivah to be named in memory of my oldest son, the talmid chacham Reb Chananya Yom Tov Lipa, Hashem yinkom damo, who was killed by the Nazis, yemach shemam, and in my opinion it would be appropriate to name the yeshivah "Ben Chayil" [an acronym of **C**hananya **Y**om Tov **L**ipa]. And see to it that you do many things to increase Torah study and glorify it.*
>
> *It is my hope that, with Hashem's help, all my friends from Klausenberg, Rudnick, and Germany who are in Eretz Yisrael will help you to be successful in this endeavor. I am confident that the merit of my holy son, who in his few short years lived a life of complete dedication to Torah and avodas Hashem, will protect the institution, and it will flourish into a large tree bearing luscious fruit, a source of pride to the Torah and those who study it.*

This and other similar acts were the Rebbe's first actions on behalf of Torah life in Eretz Yisrael, which in future years multiplied until his influence had spread to literally every corner of religious life in the Holy Land.

A Personal Emissary to Eretz Yisrael

Before the Klausenberger decided to visit Eretz Yisrael himself, he sent one of his trusted followers, Reb Yeshayah Biller, to investigate the state of affairs in the country and to determine whether it would be possible for the Rebbe to move there with a large group of his followers. The Klausenberger gave Reb Yeshayah a letter to deliver to his beloved friend in Jerusalem, Rav Avraham Getzel Shiff, in which he asked Reb Avraham Getzel to assist his emissary in every way in this endeavor. Reb Yeshayah Biller was asked to "embrace our followers who are dear to our hearts and inform us of everything you see and hear in Eretz Yisrael."

The Klausenberger later related that he sent Reb Yeshayah to the great Torah scholars of that day, the Belzer Rebbe, the Chazon Ish, and the Brisker Rav, to ask their advice and opinion on the Rebbe's plan to move to Eretz Yisrael with a large number of followers.

"From their answer," he said, "I understood that my idea was consistent with their thinking, and this encouraged me greatly. I was following in the path of the pure *rishonim*, the Rambam and the Ramban, who moved to Eretz Yisrael with great *mesirus nefesh* to till its land and rebuild its ruins. I am not afraid of the secular government [which was very fiercely opposed to religious life at the time], for it is not permanent. Hashem will soon return to His sanctuary, and they will all do *teshuvah*..."

Chapter 6

The Rebbe's First Visit to Eretz Yisrael

Preparations for the Trip

In Tishrei of 1954, the Klausenberger at long last prepared for his first visit to Eretz Yisrael. His *tefillos* during the *yamim noraim* that year were different than usual, and it was obvious that his soul was afire in anticipation of visiting the Holy Land.

During the Ten Days of Repentance, the Klausenberger wrote in a short letter to Rav Avraham Getzel Shiff, "It has now been decided that immediately after the holy *yom tov* that we will soon be celebrating I will be traveling to Eretz Yisrael." He concluded with a prayer, "May Hashem grant us the *zechus* to see the good light of our Holy Land."

During the *tisch* he held on the second day of Sukkos, the Klausenberger joyously announced, "Today we are parting from the second day of *yom tov* of *chutz la'aretz*, shortly before our departure for the Holy Land."

The anticipation of visiting Eretz Yisrael transformed the

Klausenberger into a new person. He would say in the name of his father, Reb Hershele of Rudnick, *zt"l*, that one who leaves the Diaspora and moves to Eretz Yisrael receives a new lease on life, as the seventy years allotted to a person start again from the day of one's arrival in Eretz Yisrael.

An Emotional Send-off

Due to various delays, the Klausenberger did not leave his Williamsburg home until Wednesday evening, the eighth of Cheshvan. He was accompanied by a party of ten close followers.

Before the Klausenberger left to the airport, a large crowd assembled in his *beis midrash* to receive a parting blessing and to drink a *l'chaim*. Afterwards, buses filled with hundreds of the Rebbe's followers set out for the airport, where the Rebbe was given a jubilant and emotional send-off. Song and dance broke out, and the chassidim began to sing, *"Kol rinah v'yeshuah b'ohalei tzaddikim* – the sounds of rejoicing and salvation are in the tents of the righteous."

At the height of the celebration, the Rebbe lifted his hand for a brief halt in the dancing and addressed the crowd with the following words:

"The *mefarshim* say on the verse '*T'nu oz l'Elokim* (Give strength to G-d)' that *klal Yisrael* adds strength to the Heavenly Court through their *emunah* and *bitachon* in Hashem. If we rely on and are confident in the kindness of Hashem, we add strength to the Heavenly Court. This is the meaning of the verse, "*Hashem li lo ira* (Hashem is with me, I have no fear).' When is Hashem with me? When I am not afraid of man and I have complete faith in Him."

An Unforeseen Delay

After arriving at the airport, the Klausenberger was suddenly informed that due to a change in schedule the flight would
not take off until the following morning. The Rebbe immediately told his followers that he would not leave on Thursday because it was too close to Shabbos. (At that time planes were pro-
peller driven and air travel was a long, drawn-out affair, since
there would be several stops along the way.)

The Klausenberger and his party reluctantly left the airport,
but the Rebbe did not want to return to his own home. "I am already an 'Eretz-Yisrael-dikker,' " he told his close associates. He
also had in mind the warning of Rav Yehudah HeChasid that
one should not leave his house for a trip and then return again
[if he forgot something]. Rather, he should stand in front of his
house and ask someone else to retrieve what he forgot. Therefore, the Rebbe went with his entourage to the yeshivah building
and celebrated Shabbos there with a joyous spirit and atmosphere.

Rav Shmuel Unsdorfer, who was present at the time, re-
ported, "Our Rebbe conducted himself that Shabbos with exceptional joy and undescribable excitement. How fortunate
were those who saw the Rebbe davening minchah that Friday afternoon, then dancing to welcome the Shabbos during Lechah
Dodi. How fortunate were those who participated in his tisches,
which were attended by large crowds from all over New York.

"During the Friday night meal the Rebbe gave a learned and
complex pilpul, as usual, beginning with the words of the Midrash on that week's parashah. The majority of the Rebbe's talk
focused his trip to the Holy Land, which tied in closely to the

parashah, *Parashas Lech Lecha*, and Hashem's command to Avraham, 'Go to the land which I shall show you.' There was a special spiritual elevation during *minchah* and *shalosh seudos*, when the Rebbe expressed several times his tremendous joy that he had not actually left before Shabbos, for reasons that he could not reveal."

After Shabbos, the Rebbe and his traveling party were scheduled to depart for the airport again. The Rebbe had requested that the plane not depart until after midnight because of his practice to keep Shabbos for thirty-one hours, as was the custom of the Arizal. Although the airline officials at first agreed to delay the flight departure, they later retracted and scheduled the flight for nine p.m. The Rebbe decided against traveling on this flight and instead decided to take a flight that would leave the next day.

In the Air at Last

On Sunday a large crowd gathered in the *beis midrash* of the yeshivah again to send the Rebbe off. At eleven a.m. hundreds of the Rebbe's followers, in addition to all of the yeshivah students, boarded chartered buses for the airport. After reciting *minchah* at the airport they once again sang and danced until the Rebbe boarded his flight. At last the plane took off. Upon seeing the Atlantic Ocean out the small window of the plane, the Rebbe recited the blessing "*Oseh Ma'aseh Bereishis*" with great intensity.

As the plane gathered momentum, the Rebbe turned to Rabbi Shmuel Unsdorfer and said several times, "This is no small matter! We are on our way to our Holy Land! May we merit to be worthy of receiving some of the land's holiness!"

Afterwards, they took out some food and ate, and then the Rebbe recited *Tefillas HaDerech* with great intensity.

Six hours later, the plane landed in the small airport of Gander, Newfoundland, to refuel. After a short stopover, the plane took off again and flew all night.

Tears streamed down the Rebbe's face and he prayed *maariv* on the plane. Then he studied the laws of Eretz Yisrael from the Tractate *D'mai*. During the flight he also discussed the famous halachic question of how one should treat day and night when flying over many time zones. In future years this issue and its implications interested the Rebbe a great deal, and several times he was called upon to rule on serious difficulties arising from the issue.

London

The plane landed in London at six a.m. the following morning. The Rebbe disembarked from the plane and prepared to leave the airport, since he planned on staying in London for ten days. However, his escorts explained that they had telegraphed the London Jewish community about the Rebbe's arrival, which had been scheduled for seven a.m., and they were concerned that the Rebbe's followers would be coming to the airport to greet him. After a moment's reflection, in consideration of those who might be on their way to the airport, the Rebbe agreed to wait. Sure enough, when they emerged from customs an hour later, the group was greeted by a large crowd of chassidim and Torah students, who accorded the Rebbe a royal welcome.

The Rebbe went directly to the home of Rabbi Elchanan Halpern, who was celebrating the bris of his newborn son that morning and had asked the Rebbe to be the *sandek*. The Rebbe went to immerse himself in a *mikveh* and instructed the people who had gathered in the house to daven *shacharis* without him, since he had not yet completed his preparations for *tefillah*. He did not wish to delay the bris, so he decided that he would daven afterwards, together with his fellow travelers.

After the bris the Rebbe davened *shacharis* with great intensity for several hours. The house grew more and more crowded as Jews from all over the city arrived to see him. When the Rebbe concluded his prayers, everyone streamed forward to receive his blessing. The hours passed quickly, and it was five o'clock before the Rebbe had a chance to wash his hands and sit down to partake of the *bris seudah*.

A Visit to the London Talmud Torah

On Wednesday, his third day in London, the Rebbe visited several yeshivos in London, as well as the Yesodei Torah Talmud Torah which had been established by Rabbi Shimon Shmelke Pinter. There, he lovingly but sternly rebuked the educators and requested that they not speak English to the children. He also expressed his displeasure with the length of some of the boys' hair.

At the local *mesivta*, the Klausenberger spoke movingly to the students, giving them great *chizuk*. He mentioned the famous statement of the Sages, "If this contemptible one [the evil inclination] grabs hold of you, drag him to the house of study" (*Kiddushin* 29b), and he explained that there is a *yetzer hara* to sin under the guise of *kevod Shamayim*, for example, when one interrupts his learning to speak *lashon hara*, using the pretext that one is defending the glory of Hashem. This is hinted at in the term "*menuval zeh*," since "*zeh*" is a reference to the Almighty; this contemptible one seduces one to sin by convincing him that this action will make him find favor in the eyes of his Creator. The only way to deal with this type of *yetzer hara* is to drag him into the *beis midrash* — i.e., not to step out of the four *amos* of halachah and to learn Torah in holiness and purity.

"There is no other way to do it," the Klausenberger declared. "No one knows the *yetzer hara*'s tactics better than its Creator, and if He warned us that the sole antidote for the *yetzer hara* is learning Torah, who would dare ignore this antidote and try something else?"

A Visit with the Rebbe of Shatz

During his time in London, the Rebbe visited Rav Shalom Moskowitz, the Rebbe of Shatz, who at the time was in the midst of writing a commentary on *Perek Shirah*. Reb Shalom was having difficulty understanding a particular passage in Rav Chaim Vital's *sefer Pri Etz Hadar* that was connected to his commentary and asked the Klausenberger to explain it to him.

The Klausenberger shrugged his shoulders and tried to brush the question off. "In Sanz we did not study Kabbalah," he replied.

But the elder Rebbe of Shatz persisted, "Everything your host tells you to do, you must do! I can see from your expression that you do indeed understand the passage. Please explain it to me."

Left with no choice, the Rebbe asked Reb Shalom to repeat the difficult section from *Pri Etz Chaim*. Then he rose to his feet, trembling in fear, and explained the meaning of the passage.

Speaking in Public

On Thursday night, the Rebbe was asked to speak in the Agudath Israel Beis Midrash of Rabbi Shlomo Baumgarten. Approximately five hundred people attended the *shiur*, including the rabbis and leaders of the city's religious community. Although the community had already glimpsed the Klausenberger Rebbe's greatness in Torah and his purity in prayer and deed, this *shiur* further demonstrated the depths of his knowledge and understanding, the true depths of which will never be truly measured.

The *shiur* was based on a verse in *Vayeitzei*, "And Yaakov did not know that Rachel had stolen them" (*Bereishis* 31:32). The Rebbe asked, "How is it possible that Yaakov did not know? A tzaddik like Yaakov could see the future to the end of time. It must be," he answered, "as the verse continues, that it was because Rachel stole them. A righteous woman like Rachel knew how to hide things even from Yaakov."

To explain his answer further, the Rebbe related a story about the Chozeh of Lublin, who was traveling and came to the city of Rav Mordechai of Kriminitz, the son of Rebbe Michele, the Maggid of Zlatchov. Mordechai went out to greet the Chozeh, instructing those accompanying him not to disclose his identity to the Chozeh. When they met the Chozeh's party on the outskirts of the city, the Chozeh's traveling companions asked, "Where does the tzaddik Reb Mordechai live?"

Reb Mordechai's escort told the travelers to follow them and they rode together with the Chozeh to Reb Mordechai's house. When they reached their destination, the wagon stopped, and the Chozeh asked, "Who lives here?"

Reb Mordechai, who had been riding at his side, answered, "This is my house."

The Chozeh, who was known for his ability to see hidden things, was shocked that he had not recognized Reb Mordechai. "From me you hid?" he asked in astonishment.

"We see from this," concluded the Klausenberger, "that a genuine tzaddik has the ability to hide things even from great Torah scholars to whom all hidden secrets are revealed."

It Is Time to Rebuild the Land

The Klausenberger spent that Shabbos with a large group of chassidim in a large hall that had been specially arranged for the *tefillos* and the Shabbos *tisches*. Rabbi Avraham Rand, one of the great Torah teachers in London at the time, summed up the great impact he made in the following statement: "The Rebbe's countenance on Shabbos is completely different from his countenance during the week!"

On Shabbos afternoon the Klausenberger gave a stirring speech to a large crowd, addressing the topics of educating the children in Torah, *yiras Shamayim,* and the holiness of Eretz Yisrael. He denounced the fact that religious Jewry was largely uninvolved in the rebuilding of the Holy Land.

On *motzaei Shabbos* a festive *melaveh malkah* was held in the Rebbe's honor and attended by many of the leading Jews of London. Once again, the Rebbe spoke of Eretz Yisrael and the obligation to participate in its rebuilding.

Later that night, the Rebbe met with Rav Shimon Pinter, one of the leaders of the London religious community, who gently suggested that perhaps the Klausenberger had gone too far in his comments about Eretz Yisrael. The Rebbe explained, "It seems that we religious Jews only criticize, while the irreligious are busy taking action and creating facts! I also used to criticize the nonbelievers for their actions, but my curses were not fulfilled. To the contrary, the secularists are only getting stronger. I therefore said to myself: 'Isn't it better that we switch roles — that I should build the Holy Land and they should curse me?'

"I have resolved to stop this mode of action. We will no longer stand on the side and criticize while they govern the Holy Land and defile it. We must take action to build the Holy Land! Every stone in Eretz Yisrael is pure and holy."

To Inherit the Land

In another conversation, a close follower of the Klausenberger pointed out that the irreligious original settlers in Israel, the "*chalutzim*," were the ones who had built the country, planting its fields and bringing the land back to life. The Rebbe responded with a parable about a king who chose a wife for his son. The king decided to build a beautiful palace for his son and new daughter-in-law. He bought a tract of land and imported artisans to build the palace.

Several months later, the young royal couple traveled to the location where the palace was being constructed. The workers, not recognizing them, angrily barred them from the site. The young royal couple returned to their father and complained about the treatment they had received from the construction workers. The king calmed them down, "It is true that I hired commoners to build the palace and at the moment they are in charge of the site, but as soon as the palace is completed and is turned over to me, you will be able to enter it to stay to your heart's content."

"The same is true with Eretz Yisrael," said the Rebbe. "David HaMelech said of it, 'The descendants of slaves shall inherit it and those who love His name will dwell in it' (*Tehillim* 69:36). Did you want the *b'nei Torah* to be working to build the houses and plant the fields? But the day will come when Hashem will turn the world upside down and the lovers of His Name will dwell in the land, while those who are not worthy will be ousted..."

On the Way to Eretz Yisrael

After three more days in London, the Klausenberger left for Heathrow Airport. Two hours later he landed in Paris, and from there went on to Vienna, where he had a short stopover. He davened *minchah* in a private room which was made available for him in the airport, together with a group of chassidim who came to the airport to greet him. Before boarding the plane again, the Rebbe discussed some insights into the words of the Sages, "One should not depart from his friend without first discussing words of halachah" (*Bereishis* 31a).

Continuing to Istanbul, the Rebbe davened *maariv* with a minyan on the plane. After another short stopover, a group of Sephardic *bachurim* boarded the plane. They were on their way to Eretz Yisrael to learn in Yeshivat Porat Yosef in Yerushalayim. The Rebbe took up a conversation with them and was happy to see that they were well-versed in Gemara and in the *sugyas* they were learning.

"I see," said the Rebbe happily, "that Divine Providence ensures that everyone sees exactly what he wants to see. *Baruch Hashem!* I have already at this point merited to see the best and finest of Eretz Yisrael. How beautiful is our land."

Close to midnight on Wednesday night, the plane took off, this time directly to Eretz Yisrael. Tears streamed down the Rebbe's face, his body trembled, and his lips murmured words of love for Eretz Yisrael from the *Kinnos* of Tishah B'Av, "*Tzion halo tishali... Tzion ateres tzvi... Tzion yedidos...Tzion tzefias pe'er...*"

It seemed as if the Rebbe was being accompanied to Eretz Yisrael by the angels of the Land, and the air around him was charged with the purity of the air of Eretz Yisrael.

Chapter 7

On Holy Ground

A Welcome to the Holy Land

At three-thirty a.m., the Klausenberger's plane landed at Lod Airport. As the Rebbe stepped through the door of the aircraft, cries of "*Baruch haba!*" erupted from all around. Thousands of chassidim and other followers of the Rebbe had come from all over Eretz Yisrael to welcome him. They had waited impatiently for the Rebbe's arrival for two hours, since the plane had been unexpectedly delayed.

It is not difficult to imagine the stir of emotions in the Rebbe's heart at this extraordinary moment, for which he had hoped and longed for so long, throughout the terrible years of the Holocaust — the moment when he would at last step foot on the ground of the Holy Land. The enormous emotion that gripped the thousands who came to Lod Airport that day was but a small indication of the great significance of that moment in history.

The large crowd that had gathered was made up of old and young alike, Chassidic rebbes and *roshei yeshivah*, *talmidei chachamim* and lay people — anyone with a connection to Sanz, chief among them the Holocaust survivors, who at that moment felt the sweet taste of victory over the evil Nazis.

The first to greet the Klausenberger as he descended from the plane were his longtime followers Reb Avraham Getzel Shiff and Reb Yehoshua Veitzenblum. Next after them were the leaders of the Sanz community in Yerushalayim, Reb Baruch Yitzchak Friend, Reb Mordechai Hirsch Schmerler, and Reb Chaim Hirsch Eisenbach (known as the "*chut hameshulash*," the triple-linked chain), and Reb Chaim (Hirschman) Reisher. The crowd parted so that these four elders could walk through and receive the Rebbe's blessing.

The elderly Rav Chaim Reisher made his way to the Klausenberger with firm steps. Lifting his eyes, he placed his wrinkled hand into the Klausenberger's and looked directly into the Rebbe's shining face, whispering reverently, "*Shalom aleichem*, Rebbe." Though he had never seen the Klausenberger before, having moved to Yerushalayim in 1894, eleven years before the Rebbe's birth, the Klausenberger's face was familiar to him — he looked like Rav Reisher's own rebbe, Reb Baruch of Gorlitz, the son of the Divrei Chaim. Overcome with emotion at the similarity between the Klausenberger and his great-uncle Reb Baruch of Gorlitz, Rav Chaim turned pale and almost fainted.

"I Did Not Come to Eretz Yisrael to Sleep"

The Klausenberger's face shone with light and joy, full of life and vitality. It was impossible to tell that he had not slept for two whole days. The chassidim formed a circle around him and made a path for him to enter the terminal. Once inside, the

Rebbe was greeted by thousands more who had come to see him and receive his blessing.

It was now morning, and the Klausenberger hurried to a car that was waiting to take him to Haifa, where he was to attend the bris of the newborn son of his *talmid* Rav Yaakov Bentzion Rotner. Reb Yaakov Bentzion, who was the *rav* of the Chalisah neighborhood in Haifa, had asked the Rebbe to be the *sandek* at his son's bris.

The Rebbe's first cousin Rabbi Baruch Halberstam pleaded with the Rebbe that he first come to his home in Bnei Brak and rest from his long and exhausting journey. The Rebbe, however, responded, "I did not come to Eretz Yisrael to sleep."

An Inaugural Tefillah

Immediately upon his arrival in Haifa, the Klausenberger began his preparations for his first *shacharis* in the Holy Land. He went directly to Rabbi Rotner's synagogue in Chalisah, which quickly filled with people from all over Haifa. The Rebbe's davening that morning was a new experience even for his traveling party, who were used to his way of prayer, for this *shacharis* was completely different than any he had ever davened before.

This was the inauguration of the Rebbe's seven weeks in Eretz Yisrael — seven weeks of light and joy, during which the entire religious population of Eretz Yisrael basked under his influence. During these seven weeks the Rebbe was completely consumed, day and night, with bringing honor to the Creator and His Torah. It is difficult to determine when the Rebbe slept, if he slept at all, during his entire stay.

Visiting the Belzer Rebbe

After *shacharis* and the bris, the Rebbe traveled to Tel Aviv to greet the Belzer Rebbe, Reb Aharon Rokeach. He had sent Rav Shmuel Unsdorfer and Rav Yehoshua Veitzenblum to Tel Aviv earlier to arrange a time to meet with this chassidic giant. The Belzer Rebbe had warmly inquired about the Klausenberger's trip and about his plans for the coming days, and then told them that he was planning to conduct a *tisch* that evening in honor of the *yahrtzeit* of his father, the previous Belzer Rebbe, and it would be better if the Klausenberger came after the *tisch*, at nine p.m. (Afterwards, he amended this by saying that if the Klausenberger arrived early he should not be concerned, because the Belzer Rebbe would interrupt the *tisch* to greet him.) The two rebbes were longtime friends, since whenever the Klausenberger had visited the previous Belzer Rebbe, Rav Yissachar Dov, *zt"l*, in his youth, he would always eat a meal at his son Reb Aharon's house.

At 9 p.m. that evening, the Klausenberger arrived at the Belzer Rebbe's home. Reb Aharon came to the entrance of his home to greet his guest and led him into his private study, seating the Klausenberger beside him at the head of the table. The Klausenberger, however, moved his seat to the side of the table, sitting humbly like a student before his teacher.

The two great rebbes began to discuss a number of significant issues, particularly issues relating to Eretz Yisrael. The Klausenberger's party was present in the room only for a short time, and thus heard only a small part of the conversation.

The Belzer Rebbe opened the conversation by asking how the Klausenberger had reached Eretz Yisrael. When the Rebbe replied that he had arrived by plane, Reb Aharon said, "At one point I was very concerned about traveling by plane. Then I thought to myself, Perhaps it is better to travel by plane because traveling by ship causes too much *bitul Torah*. I decided to travel by plane, but it seems to me that one should not recite the blessing of *HaGomel* with *Shem U'Malchus* after a plane trip."

(Although the Klausenberger ruled that one should recite *Birkas HaGomel* after plane travel, he refrained from reciting it on that trip because of the Belzer Rebbe's comment. In a later trip to Eretz Yisrael, the Rebbe sailed to Paris by boat and then flew from there to Eretz Yisrael so that he could recite *Birkas HaGomel* with Hashem's name even according to the Belzer Rebbe.)

Afterwards, the Klausenberger told the Belzer Rebbe that when trains were first invented his great-grandfather, the Divrei Chaim, had said jokingly, "Surely this is preparation for the coming of Mashiach, when only complete tzaddikim will be *zocheh* to come to Eretz Yisrael on the *ananei hakavod*. Everyone else will have to come by train!" It would seem, he continued, that planes were also created for this purpose, to enable the Jewish people to reach Eretz Yisrael more quickly.

Reb Aharon's face lit up when he heard this and he responded, "As you say. As you say. All the planes are a preparation for the coming of the Mashiach and the ingathering of *am Yisrael*, may it happen speedily."

During the course of the visit, the Belzer Rebbe's assistant served the two great leaders cake and schnapps for a *l'chaim*. Reb Aharon placed the food and drink in front of the Klausenberger so that he should eat first, but the Klausenberger pushed the food back to his host, telling him to eat first. Reb Aharon cut a large piece of cake and offered it to the Rebbe, explaining, "Here in Belz we are very strict with regard to the size of a *kezayis*."

They drank a *l'chaim* and Reb Aharon praised the drink highly, since it was a banana liquor made from fruit of Eretz Yisrael. The Klausenberger told him, "That this drink has been placed on a holy table is enough in and of itself."

Afterwards, the two great men were served a plate of Israeli fruit, and they discussed the significance of the fruits of Eretz Yisrael, whose ingestion can increase a person's spiritual level.

At the conclusion of the visit, the Belzer Rebbe escorted the Klausenberger to the door, and the two giants wished each other farewell with great love and affection. The Klausenberger returned to Haifa, where he stayed for a short rest. Even before sunrise, however, he rose and set out for the holy city of Tzefas.

The Rebbe's Arrival in Tzefas

The Klausenberger was drawn to the city of Tzefas as if by a magnetic force. His initial letter to Rabbi Avraham Getzel Shiff revealing his plans to come to Eretz Yisrael concluded with the terse statement, "My trip is to the city of Tzefas." According to one report, the Rebbe was planing to settle there. In later years, he was heard to say, "If people were able to see how every stone in Tzefas shines like the afternoon sun, they would flock to it from all over the world."

The Kabbalist Rav Avraham Azulai, grandfather of the Chida, said about this city, "There is no place in all of Eretz Yisrael with air as clear and as pure as the air of Tzefas." According to the scholars of old, Tzefas is located directly beneath the Divine Throne. Students of Kabbalah, quoting the great Rav Mordechai of Kriminitz, long ago instructed that at the very least "one's first residence in the Holy Land should be in the city of Tzefas."

Passing by the town of Meron on the way to Tzefas, the Rebbe's driver, thinking that the Klausenberger would surely want to stop at the grave of Rabbi Shimon bar Yochai, drove into the town. The Rebbe, however, was very upset and had the driver turn around, saying that he could not visit the grave without adequate preparations.

The Klausenberger entered the narrow streets of Tzefas through a gate erected especially in his honor. He went directly to the *mikveh* and immersed himself, and then walked quickly to the old Sanz *beis midrash* in the city to daven *shacharis*. This *beis midrash* had been founded under the instruction of the Divrei Chaim of Sanz in 1870, some eighty-five years before, when the Divrei Yechezkel of Shinov visited Eretz Yisrael. The Divrei Chaim had said that since all the *tefillos* of the Jewish people pass through Eretz Yisrael on their way to the heavens above, he wanted to have his own *beis midrash* in the holy city of Tzefas through which his prayers would ascend on high. Chassidim of earlier generations would say that the letters of the name *Tzefas* were an acronym for "*Tzanz po takum* — Sanz will be built here."

Standing in this very *beis midrash*, the Klausenberger poured his heart out to the Almighty with cries and groans that undoubtedly pierced the heavens above.

The Rebbe in the early years after liberation

The Rebbe after liberation

Rav Shmuel Ungar, the Rebbe's father-in-law

Rav Michael Ber Weissmandel, the Rebbe's brother-in-law

Rav Yaakov Kaminetzky visiting the Rebbe in his summer camp

The old *yeshivah ketanah* building in Williamsburg

The Klausenberg *beis midrash* in Williamsburg

The Sanz-Klausenberg *beis midrash* in Boro Park

The Klausenberg yeshivah building in Boro Park

The Sanz-Klausenberg building on Bedford Avenue

The new Bais Chana building in Williamsburg

The Rebbe in his summer camp in Woodridge in 1964,
shown with Reb Binyamin Williger and Reb Nesanel Tzvi Wax

The Sanz-Klausenberg yeshivah building in Union City, N.J.

Vacation apartments in the summer camp in the mountains

The Rebbe personally inspecting the *mikveh* in one of the summer camps.
At his right is his *mechutan*, Rav Aharon Wieder.

לבזל טוב

אתכבד בזה לחזמין את מע״כ להשתתף בשמחה של מצוה
יום כלילת ח״ב המו״מ בתורה ויראת שמים

כמר אלעזר קרעניגום נ״י

בן מו״ה אברהם אביש האגער ז״ל הי״ד
מאויבער-וויטא, נכד הגאה״ק טקאטוב ומראפשיץ ומסאסוב זי״ע
תלמיד חביב בישיבתנו ראשית חכמה ושא״ם

עב״ג הבתולה הכלה החמודה

מרת מרים נאלדא תחי׳

בת הרב וכו׳ מו״ה יצחק הלוי קלייז שליט״א

אשר תחי׳ אי״ה בשעה טובה ומוצלחת

ביום ה׳ נצבים-וילך, כ״א לחודש אלול, הבע״ל
בשעה 8:00 בערב

באולם ראיאל מענאר

175 האדרם סטריט, ברוקליז, נ. י.

והשי״ת ישפיע להם שפעת חיים ושלום וכל טוב סלה

ונזכה לגאולת עולם בב״א

ח״ק יקותיאל יהודה הלבערשטאם
כלפנים אבדק״ק קלייזענבורג

An invitation to the wedding of one of the Rebbe's *talmidim*,
Reb Eliezer Hager

The Rebbe participating in the *badeken* of a *talmid's* wedding

The Rebbe at the *kever* of Rabbi Shimon bar Yochai in Meron

The Rebbe in the ancient cemetery in Tzefas, together with Reb Yechezkel Shraga Frankel, Reb Yechezkel Roth, and the Ziditchover Rebbe (at the far left)

Jerusalem residents escorting the Rebbe on his first visit to the city

The Rebbe davening at the Kosel

The Rebbe on his arrival in Eretz Yisrael

The Rebbe reciting *Krias Shema* on an airplane

The Rebbe speaking at the cornerstone-laying ceremony of Kiryat Sanz

The Rebbe making a *l'chaim* upon putting up mezuzos in his home in Kiryat Sanz. On his right is Reb Yechezkel Neuwirth, the Rebbe's right-hand man in the building project.

The Rebbe speaking in the Meah Shearim Yeshivah in Jerusalem.
At his left is Rav Shmuel Unsdorfer. Near the pillar on the right is
Reb Avraham Getzel Shiff.

The Rebbe reading from the Torah
at the *kever* of Rabbi Shimon bar Yochai in Meron

The *chanukas habayis* of the Beis Yaakov HaYashan in Jerusalem

The Rebbe sitting with Reb Yechezkel Reich, one of his closest followers throughout his years in America

An Exalted Revelation

After *shacharis*, the Rebbe went to the home of his host, Reb Shimon Diamond, and began to prepare for the upcoming Shabbos. The excitement and anticipation among the Jews of Tzefas grew by the hour. It was obvious that the city was about to experience a Shabbos the likes of which it had not experienced in a very long time. In honor of the Rebbe's arrival, many important and respected chassidim of Sanz and Sighet arrived in Tzefas from all over the country. As the sun set, the Rebbe made his way to the synagogue of the Arizal for *Kabbalas Shabbos*. According to Kabbalistic tradition, this shul was built in the location known as *Chakal Tapuchin Kadishin*, "the holy apple tree," and this was where the Arizal and his *talmidim* came every Friday to welcome the Shabbos Queen.

Arriving at the shul, the Klausenberger stopped in the doorway and stood perfectly still, his eyes closed and his face shining brightly. Later, he related the extraordinary vision that he had at the time: "At that very moment, the Creator enabled me to feel and actually see the holiness of Eretz Yisrael. I saw that it would be good for me to live here, and it was then that I decided to move to Eretz Yisrael as soon as possible."

During that entire Shabbos, the Rebbe radiated a special joy and holiness, both in his prayers and at his *tisches*, which were held in a large hall next to the Arizal's shul. The hundreds of chassidim present overflowed with joy in the hope that the Sanz dynasty would at last be rebuilt in Eretz Yisrael.

Visiting the She'eiris HaPleitah Institutions

After Shabbos, the Klausenberger remained in Tzefas for three more days. Learned and simple Jews alike lined up at the house where he was staying to receive his blessing and seek his advice. Community leaders came to speak with him about how to strengthen religious observance and Torah education in Tzefas and the surrounding areas. The Rebbe also visited the local institutions under his auspices, the Yesodei HaTorah elementary school and the Bais Yaakov.

As night fell on Tuesday of *Parashas Toldos*, the twenty-seventh of Cheshvan, 1955, the Rebbe bid an emotional farewell to the Jews of Tzefas. In response to their entreaties, he promised to return to the city for another Shabbos during his stay in the Holy Land. Then he drove towards the center of the country, stopping in Bnei Brak before he continued south to Yerushalayim.

In Bnei Brak the Rebbe first went to visit his dear friend the Vizhnitzer Rebbe, the Imrei Chaim, who welcomed him with great honor and excitement. The Klausenberger expressed great interest in the construction of Kiryat Vizhnitz. The Vizhnitzer Rebbe told him that some sixty-eight families were already living in the community. "A new community of sixty-eight pure and pious families in Eretz Yisrael is no small matter," the Rebbe commented. "May it only continue!"

After his visit with the Imrei Chaim, the Rebbe attended the engagement party of a *talmid* from the Foehrenwald DP camp, Chaim Alter Roth. He spoke in honor of the occasion and was as joyous as if he was the *chasan*'s father. However, when he was offered a plate of fruit, he declined, explaining that he had not yet had the opportunity to analyze all the applicable laws of *terumos* and *maasros*.

Upon leaving the city the next day, the Rebbe stopped for a brief visit in Azor, where his students had established a She'eiris HaPleitah elementary school under his direction. Then he continued to Yerushalayim.

In Your Gates, Yerushalayim

Hundreds of Yerushalmi Jews poured into the narrow streets of Motza, at the outskirts of the city, to welcome the Rebbe to the city. From there he traveled in a motorcade to the Sephardic Orphanage Home on Jaffa Road, in the heart of the city, where thousands more waited to get a glimpse of him. After an enthusiastic welcome, the Klausenberger davened *maariv* in the hall, beginning, as usual, with his recital of *Shir HaMaalos*. Suddenly, when he reached the last verse, "*Mi yitein miTzion yeshuas Yisrael* — Oh, that out of Zion shall come the salvation of Israel," he was once again ignited by fire. In a heartrending wail, he repeated the verse again and again: "*Mi yitein, mi yitein miTzion, oy vey Tatte, mi yitein yeshuas Yisrael...*"

The great *gaon* and chassid Rav Chanoch Henoch Padwa (author of *Cheishev Eifod* and the head of the London *beis din*, who was present at the time) later said, "Today I learned for the first time that the verses of *Shir HaMaalos* recited before *maariv* are a prayer in and of themselves."

After *maariv* the enormous crowd escorted the Rebbe to the home of Rabbi Avraham Yaakov Osebal on Rechov Levush Mordechai, where he would be staying. Over the next several weeks hundreds of people streamed to this apartment to seek

the Klausenberger's advice and blessing, while mountains of
kvittlach piled up on the table in front of him.

"To You I Shall Offer Sacrifices"

On the following day, the Rebbe davened *shacharis* in the
Chassidim Shul in Batei Varshah. The synagogue filled quickly
as word of the Klausenberger's appearance spread. The congregation listened, teary-eyed, to the Rebbe's emotional prayers, especially when he reached the verse, "*Eizehu mekomam shel
zevachim* — Which is the place of sacrifices?" All who were present felt the pain of the Klausenberger's piercing question:
"Where is the place of sacrifices today? When will the Beis
HaMikdash be rebuilt? Hasn't there been enough destruction
and suffering for the Jewish people and for the Shechinah,
which is in exile with us?"

On the following day, Friday, Rosh Chodesh Kislev, a large
crowd gathered once again to hear the Rebbe's *tefillos*. The congregation stood watching, absorbing every word he uttered, for
four solid hours. The Rebbe's intensity peaked with *Hallel*, as he
paced back and forth in front of the holy ark, his hands lifted towards the heavens, singing over and over again, "*Lecha ezbach
zevach todah...negdah na l'chol amo... B'chatzros beis Hashem,
b'socheichi Yerushalayim...* To You I will sacrifice thanksgiving
offerings...in the presence now, of His entire people... In the
courtyards of the House of Hashem, in your midst, O Jerusalem."

Shabbos in Yerushalayim

Shabbos Parashas Toldos was the Rebbe's first Shabbos in Yerushalayim. The city was buzzing with the excitement over the Rebbe's visit, and thousands assembled in Yeshivas Meah Shearim, where the Rebbe davened all the *tefillos*, his piercing voice echoing throughout the *beis midrash*, to hear his davening.

Holocaust survivors from Hungary and Romania crowded around their beloved Rebbe, sobbing as they listened to his powerful voice. The elder Sanz chassidim who had lived in Yerushalayim for generations were entranced by the sound of the Rebbe's prayers, which reminded them of the melodies they had heard as children in their fathers' homes. The Klausenberger prayed with his entire being, as if his life was dependent on each word. As was his way, he repeated the words *"V'haer eineinu b'Sorasecha,* Enlighten our eyes in Your Torah," in the blessings of Shema over and over again.

The Rebbe's *tisches* that Shabbos, held in the dining room of the Chayei Olam Yeshivah in Kikar Shabbos, were also attended by thousands, many of whom hung on to the walls and rafters just to catch a glimpse of the Rebbe. The Rebbe spoke to their souls with inspiring words of Torah and haunting melodies. He groaned and cried as he sang, *"Tzavei yeshuos Yaakov,* Command the salvation of Yaakov..." and *"L'Mikdasheich tuv u'lekodesh kudshin,* To Your sanctuary return and to the Holy of Holies... Where they will utter songs and praises to You, in Yerushalayim, city of beauty."

To the Klausenberger's close followers, there was nothing new in the Rebbe's prayers and melodies, but they, too, sensed a special quality and a heightened intensity in the Rebbe's service

in Yerushalayim, the palace of the King. But for those who had
never met the Rebbe before, his approach to *avodas Hashem* was
a glimpse into Gan Eden. As Rav Shmuel Unsdorfer recalled,
"Everyone was awed by the extraordinary scene, the likes of
which they had never witnessed before."

These scenes were repeated on the following Shabbos,
Parashas Vayeitzei, which the Rebbe also spent in Yerushalayim,
before an even larger crowd.

The Ushpitzin Beis Midrash

During the weekdays the Rebbe prayed in the *beis midrash*
of Rav Eliezer Rosenfeld of Ushpitzin, located in Meah Shearim
opposite Batei Verner. Reb Eliezer, son of Rav Yehoshua of
Kaminka and a son-in-law of the Divrei Chaim, had lived in
Yerushalayim from 1936 to 1939. When World War II broke
out, he suddenly traveled back to Ushpitzin, leaving his wife behind in Yerushalayim, and was trapped in the Nazi furor. He
was killed *al kiddush haShem*, together with the entire Jewish
community of Ushpitzin, the town which eventually became the
site of the concentration camp of Auschwitz.

The Sanz chassidim in Yerushalayim, followers of the
Divrei Chaim, had turned to Reb Eliezer for guidance during his
entire stay in Yerushalayim. After his departure, the small group
continued to gather in his *beis midrash* and daven there. Chief
among them was Rabbi Yosef Shmuel Frankel, whom Reb
Eliezer had appointed *gabbai* of the *beis midrash*. After the war,
when Reb Yosef Shmuel heard that the Klausenberger Rebbe
had survived the war, he and others decided to turn to him for
spiritual guidance. Reb Yosef Shmuel and his young sons con-

tinued to try to strengthen the Ushpitzin *beis midrash*, gathering together a group of chassidim who developed their connection with the Rebbe from afar and eagerly looked forward to the day when they would meet the Rebbe in person.

Now their dream had come true — the Rebbe had arrived in Yerushalayim! Select members of the Ushpitzin *beis midrash* went to greet the Rebbe and ask to be taken under his wing. Among these members were Rav Yosef Shmuel Frankel and his two sons, Yechezkel Shraga and Naftali; Rabbi Yaakov Shtemmer and his son Tzvi; Rabbi Eliyahu Shmuel Schmerler (the present *rosh yeshivah* of the Sanz yeshivah in Kiryat Sanz); Rabbi Naftali Genger; Rabbi Yaakov Shaul Weinfeld, and Rabbis Naftali and Moshe Halberstam (sons of Rabbi Yaakov Halberstam, *zt"l*, and grandsons of Rabbi Sinai of Zemigrad). The Rebbe conversed with them at length regarding the holy ways of Sanz Chassidus, and when he saw that they were true followers of the Divrei Chaim he agreed to accept them as his chassidim.

These were the first seeds of Sanz Chassidus in the Holy Land — seeds which eventually developed into an enormous network of shuls and yeshivos, and even entire communities.

Visiting Great Torah Leaders in Yerushalayim

During the Klausenberger's stay in Yerushalayim, he was driven to Talpiyot, in the southern part of the city, from which one could see the Temple Mount, which was then under Jordanian rule. Upon seeing the Temple Mount, the Rebbe tore his clothes and wept. He sat and gazed at the mountain for a long time, tears streaming down his face as he mourned the destruction of the holy Temple.

While in Yerushalayim, the Rebbe also made courtesy calls on many of the great Torah scholars living there at the time, including the Gerrer Rebbe, the Beis Yisrael; the Tchebiner Rav, Rav Dov Berish Widenfeld (author of the *Dovev Meisharim*); the Brisker Rav, Rabbi Yitzchak Zev Soloveitchik; the Pressburger Rav, Rav Akiva Sofer; Rabbi Pinchas Epstein, head of the *beis din* of the Eidah HaChareidis; the great scholar from Brashuv, Rabbi David Shparber; and Rabbi Yisrael Zev Mintzberg, who had been the head of the chassidic *beis din* of the Old City. Many great Torah scholars and chassidic rebbes came to pay their respects to the Rebbe as well.

When he met with the Brisker Rav, Reb Velvel Soloveitchik, the Klausenberger repeated a Torah insight which he had heard from the latter many years before at a *shiur* the latter had given in Warsaw. Despite all that the Klausenberger had been through since the *shiur*, he had not forgotten this Torah insight and repeated it in precise detail.

When their discussion turned to the spiritual state of the Jewish people, the Rebbe said, "Now that I am here and can see up close what is happening, I can better understand the words of *Chazal*, 'Whoever walks four cubits in Eretz Yisrael merits a share in the World to Come' (*Kesubos* 11a). It is so true. There is so much to do here to honor the Creator that with every step one takes he can merit the World to Come. Mitzvos come with every step — you don't even have to search for them."

When the Klausenberger visited the Gerrer Rebbe, the Rebbe was waiting for him at the door and welcomed him with grand honor. They met privately and spoke confidentially for a long time.

The Story of the Tchebiner Gaon

When the Rebbe visited with the Tchebiner Gaon, Rav Dov Berish Widenfeld, they spoke for a long time about chassidim of earlier generations. The Tchebiner, who was a descendant of the Rozhin and Tchortkov dynasties, told the Klausenberger a story about the famous *gaon* Rabbi Meir Arak, author of the *Imrei Yosher*, whom the Rebbe had known in his youth.

Reb Meir would tremble at the mere mention of his rebbe, the saintly Tchortkover Rebbe, Reb Dovid Moshe. However, when Reb Meir assumed his rabbinic responsibilities, his true strength of character was revealed. He was once serving as the *rav* of Yazlovitch, a town on the outskirts of Tchortkov, and a poor, simple Jew came before him with a significant monetary claim against the Tchortkover Rav. After learning the basic nature of the claims, Rav Meir dispatched his *shamash* to serve a summons on the Tchortkover Rebbe, asking him to attend the *din Torah*.

Reb Meir's assistant arrived at the courtyard of the Tchortkover Rebbe speechless with fear. He finally managed to stammer out a few words, explaining that he was there to deliver a summons to the Rebbe.

The Rebbe's followers were astounded. "What has happened to the rabbi from Yazlovitch? Does a king get summoned to court? Who is this person who dared speak ill of the holy Rebbe, claiming that he caused him harm?"

The Tchortkover, however, took the matter quite seriously and accepted the summons. Quieting his followers, he appointed a faithful chassid as his spokesperson and sent him with a power of attorney to represent him in the *din Torah*. "Jus-

tice belongs to the Almighty," said the Tchortkover Rebbe. "I
will follow the *beis din*'s ruling."

On the Shabbos after the *din Torah*, Reb Meir went to
Tchortkov to spend Shabbos with his rebbe. The entire Shabbos,
the Tchortkover Rebbe went out of his way to display his love for
Reb Meir, according him great honor for all to see. "They said in
Tchortkov that there was a connection between the events," explained the Tchebiner Rav. "The Tchortkover Rebbe intended to
demonstrate publicly that not only did he not bear the slightest
grudge against Reb Meir, but also his admiration for Reb Meir
and his Torah had grown. For Reb Meir fulfilled the verse, 'And
you shall not be afraid of man, for judgment belongs to the Almighty.' "

The Klausenberger loved this story and repeated it from
time to time as an example of the ways of the great Torah scholars of old.

Modest Beginnings

The day before the Klausenberger left Yerushalayim, a group
of chassidim who wished to accept his leadership gathered and
presented the Rebbe with a written document of their intentions:
"We have gathered together, followers of the Rebbe, in the presence of our Rebbe, the *gaon* of Klausenberg, *shlita*, to establish for
his followers a *beis midrash* in the traditions of Sanz and to join together as a community in which each one will help strengthen the
others, under the advice, blessing, and leadership of the Rebbe.
We will act according to his word, and we will live in his shadow,
until the coming of Mashiach, speedily in our days."

Among those present were Reb Mordechai Tzvi Schmerler;

Reb Baruch Yitzchak Friend; Reb Chaim Reisher; the Chernobler Rebbe, Rabbi Meshulam Zusha Twersky (grandson of Rabbi Yeshayah of Tchekov-Krakow, the youngest son of the Divrei Chaim); Reb Yosef Shmuel Frankel and his sons; his brother Reb Mendel Frankel; Reb Yehoshua Veitzenblum; Reb Pesach langsam; Reb Dovid Greenzweig; Reb Moshe Reichman; Reb Moshe Walter; Reb Tzvi Green; and Reb Yaakov Shaul Weinfeld.

Following this meeting, the first Klausenberger *beis midrash* in Eretz Yisrael was established in the heart of Yerushalayim, near Kikar Shabbos. The *beis midrash* was named "Heichal Tzvi" in memory of the Rebbe's father, Reb Tzvi Hirsch of Rudnick.

A Tour of the South

On Wednesday, the thirteenth of Kislev, the Rebbe finally left Yerushalayim. Outside the city he visited a religious Yemenite community, Eshtaol, whose residents lived in dire poverty, their clothes torn and ragged. Their difficult circumstances made a deep impression on the Klausenberger, as did their synagogues, Torah scrolls, and *mikveh*.

Next on the Rebbe's itinerary was the town of Yesodot in Nachal Sorek, where he found a beautiful community of religious farmers with a *talmud Torah* for the children. After a short visit in the home of Rav Ben Tzion Klein, the Rebbe continued on his way and visited the city of Yavneh, where he was able to see the Ben Chayil Yeshivah, named after his son Liepele, for the first time.

The Rebbe then visited the religious moshav of Beit Chilkiyah, where again he found religious, G-d-fearing settlers.

Rabbi Yosef Zimmerman, a former student of the Brisker Yeshivah in Tashnad, Transylvania, who served as the *rav* of Beit Chilkiyah, asked the Klausenberger for suggestions on how to improve the community. The Klausenberger responded that the children should be taught in Yiddish and that Torah studies should be taught in the morning and secular studies in the afternoon.

After Beit Chilkiyah, the Rebbe visited Moshav Bnei Ra'am, where he met with the local *rav*, Rabbi Nachman Kahana, a grandson of the Imrei Yosef of Spinka. The Rebbe was very pleased to see fifty children learning Torah in the traditional Yiddish on this *moshav*.

From there the Rebbe traveled to Komemiyus, a religious farming community of approximately eighty families. The moshav was run completely according to halachah, under the leadership of Rav Binyamin Mendelson, a Gerrer chassid.

From Komemiyus the Rebbe traveled to Migdal Gad, and from there to Ashkelon, where he davened *maariv* and spoke to the congregation. He stayed overnight in Ashkelon, at the home of the local *rav*, Rabbi Wolner.

Early the next morning, the Rebbe left for Be'er Sheva, where he davened *shacharis*. In the afternoon, he traveled north to the capitol of the Galilee region, Tzefas, where he planned to spend the upcoming Shabbos, *Parashas Vayishlach*.

When the Rebbe arrived in Tzefas with his entourage, he was once again greeted by the city's leaders, who viewed his visit as bringing new glory and beauty to their city. Once again, hundreds of people came to celebrate Shabbos with the Rebbe and to experience a Shabbos as he experienced it. The davening and *tisch*es were held in the Arizal's shul. Once again, the dancing and singing during *Kabbalas Shabbos* and the inspiring *divrei Torah* lifted the assembled to awesome new spiritual heights. Parting from this Shabbos was very difficult for all those present.

Visiting the Ancient Cemetery of Tzefas

On Sunday morning, the seventeenth of Kislev, the Rebbe davened *shacharis* in the second *beis midrash* of the Arizal, adjacent to the old cemetery of Tzefas. He became very emotional when he entered the small outer room of the *beis midrash*, where, according to tradition, the Arizal had learned Kabbalah with Eliyahu HaNavi. Perhaps he was able to sense the Divine light which emanated from the walls of the tiny room. To those present that morning, the Rebbe expressed his wonderment at how the Arizal had managed to learn Torah in such dire poverty, sitting in the tiny room without even a window for light or ventilation.

After *shacharis* the Rebbe went to pray at the graves of the tzaddikim buried in the old cemetery of Tzefas, including the *Tanna* Rabbi Pinchas ben Yair, the Arizal, the Ramak, the Beis Yosef, the Alshich, Rabbi Moshe the son of the Ari, Rabbi Elazar Azkari, author of *Chareidim*, Rabbi Moshe Alkabetz, and others. He recited *Tehillim* with great emotion, weeping the entire time. When he reached the grave of the Arizal, he stood barefoot for a long time, his hands lifted to the heavens, tears streaming silently down his face. Afterwards he prostrated himself completely on the gravestone. At the grave of his ancestor the Toltsheva Rebbe, Rav Moshe David Ashkenazi, he cried for a long time, davening for the redemption of *klal Yisrael.*

Amukah and Rabbi Yehudah bar Ila'i

Later that day, the Klausenberger visited the tomb of Rabbi Yonasan ben Uziel in the Amukah valley near Tzefas. Since there were no paved roads to the tomb at the time, the Rebbe reached it by donkey, enduring the uncomfortable ride with a smile on his face.

As night approached, the Rebbe returned to Tzefas. On the outskirts of the city, he passed the grave of the *Tanna* Rabbi Yehudah bar Ila'i and stopped there to recite *minchah.* As he concluded his *tefillos* and continued on his way, the chassidim noted with concern that the Klausenberger was crying bitterly. When questioned, however, the Rebbe refused to explain the reason for his tears.

The following day, when the Rebbe was in Meron, he asked to be taken again to the grave of Rabbi Yehudah bar Ila'i. There he davened *minchah* for a very long time, crying bitterly.

When he had finished, his entourage saw that his face was now calm and at peace. Reb Shmuel Unsdorfer asked the Rebbe about his change of mood.

"As we were returning to Tzefas yesterday," the Rebbe explained, "I reviewed the events of the day and suddenly realized that Rabbi Yehudah bar Ila'i was the *tanna* who taught that the time for reciting *minchah* is only until *plag haminchah.* How could I have davened at his grave after the time that he held was the proper time to pray? I was shattered and could not compose myself. Today we returned to his grave and I made sure to daven *minchah* before *plag haminchah.* Then I asked the holy *tanna* for forgiveness for unintentionally praying at his grave at a time inconsistent with his opinion, and I begged Hashem for forgiveness for this grave error."

Meron

Early Monday morning, the Klausenberger set out for the tomb of Rabbi Shimon bar Yochai in Meron. Entering the tomb with a spirit of great awe, he davened *shacharis* with deep concentration. Upon reaching the verses "*Ya'alzu chassidim b'chavod, yeromemu al mishkevosam,* Let the devout exult in glory, let them sing joyously upon their beds," he began to cry, repeating each word over and over. Tears streamed down the faces of all who were present.

After *shacharis* an elderly Jew from the area approached the Klausenberger with the following plea: "Rebbe, please arouse the mercy of Heaven. *Klal Yisrael* is in desperate need of a salvation."

The Klausenberger responded, "We can rely on Rabbi Shimon bar Yochai in times of need. His great merit will stand by all of the Jews in this holy land."

Leaving the tomb of Rabbi Shimon bar Yochai, the Rebbe went to daven at the graves of the other *tannaim* and *amora'im* buried in the area. He even climbed the stony terrain to the site known as the Seat of Eliyahu. At the top of the mountain, at the grave of Rabbi Yochanan HaSandlar, the Rebbe noticed a large sign which displayed several Talmudic statements of this *tanna*. He immediately gave his entourage an explanation and *pilpul* on the passages, drawing connections between the seemingly disparate quotes displayed on the sign.

The day was etched in the memories of all who traveled with the Klausenberger as one of the most significant days of the Rebbe's visit to Eretz Yisrael. As he himself said upon leaving the tomb of Rabbi Shimon bar Yochai in the morning, "All the pain and torture I endured in my lifetime were worth suffering just for the opportunity to visit Meron once in my lifetime."

Chapter 8

In the Galil and the Negev

To the Cradle of Chassidus

On Tuesday, the nineteenth of Kislev, the Klausenberger left Tzefas for Teveriah, the cradle of Chassidus in Eretz Yisrael at that time. The *rabbanim* and leaders of the ancient city prepared a royal welcome for him. The Rebbe emerged from the car on his arrival and walked forward hesitantly, saying, "How can I walk on the holy ground of Teveriah, which is perhaps the only place on earth that is called 'holy ground'?"

Continuing to the home of his host, Rabbi Meir Halberstam, a descendant of Sanz, the Rebbe was warmly welcomed by a welcoming party which included Rabbi Asher Zev Werner, the local *rav*; the Slonimer Rebbe, Reb Avraham, who was known as the Birkas Avraham; and Chacham Yaakov Chai Zerihan and Chacham Meir Veknin, the rabbis of the city's Sephardic community. Also present were the elders of the chassidic community, including the Rebbe's relative Rabbi Yoel Ashkenazi, a grandson of the Toltsheva Rebbe; Rabbi Menachem Mendel Weg; Rabbi Aharon Yosef Luria, author of

Avodas Penim; and Rabbi Yitzchak Matisyahu Luria, a *rosh yeshivah* in Yeshivas Ohr Torah.

The Rebbe exchanged warm greetings with all of them and discussed the state of religious life in Teveriah. Then he davened *maariv* in a very emotional state, to the awe of his guests, who had never before witnessed such an intense prayer on a regular weekday.

Late that night, the Rebbe's host Rabbi Meir Halberstam brought him a cup of water for washing his hands in the morning, thinking that the Klausenberger was certainly going to sleep for several hours after a full day of travel and meetings. When he saw the light in the Rebbe's room still burning, however, he peeked in and saw the Klausenberger lying prostrate on the floor. He stood in awe, listening to the Rebbe's recital of *kerias Shema* for close to an hour.

Repairing the Mikveh

The remaining hours of the night passed quickly. When the sun rose the next morning, the Klausenberger went to immerse himself in an ancient *mikveh* that was situated at the end of a narrow, winding street that adjoined the Kinneret. Beneath a large courtyard known as "the Azarah," in which the Sephardic Great Synagogue of Teveriah and three other ancient synagogues were located, was an underground spring that flowed from the Kinneret. According to tradition, the Arizal would immerse in this spring and pray there, too. Later, when the ancient *mikveh* that he had used had collapsed, it was rebuilt in the standard fashion, with a pool of water connected to the water source with a pipe.

When the Klausenberger entered the *mikveh*, he did not like how the pipe was connected to the water source and immediately asked to speak to the person responsible for the *mikveh*. When the man appeared, the Rebbe instructed him to repair the pipe immediately, following specific directives, and promised to pay for the work himself, following the Talmudic adjunct to "prepare *mikva'os* for every day" (*Shabbos* 33b).

The man, who was well-versed in halachah, responded that the *mikveh* was actually kosher, so what was all the fuss about? The Rebbe responded, "All my life I have never eaten a food that is only kosher *bedi'eved*. I have never worn tzitzis that met just the minimal kashrus standards. Should I be satisfied with a *mikveh* that requires a scholar's approval to be kosher?"

In the end, the Rebbe asked his host Reb Meir to supervise the repair and not leave Teveriah until it was done. Even though Reb Meir very much desired to spend the coming Shabbos with the Rebbe in Be'er Sheva, he obeyed the Rebbe's command remained in Teveriah and remained in Teveriah. When the repairs to the *mikveh* were completed that Friday, he sent a telegram to this effect to the Rebbe. The Rebbe later thanked him for the telegram, saying, "You brightened my entire Shabbos!"

At the Grave of the Rambam

After immersing himself, the Klausenberger davened *shacharis* at Yeshivas Ohr Torah, overlooking the Kinneret, alongside the grave of Rabbi Meir Ba'al HaNess. Everyone present listened attentively to every word he recited for close to two hours.

Afterwards, many of the chassidim of Teveriah came to

place *kvittlach* in the Rebbe's hand, asking for his prayers and blessings. The Klausenberger also used his time in the city to daven at the graves of the *tannaim* and *amoraim* and other great tzaddikim that were buried there, among them the Rambam and the Shelah.

Before he went to the gravesite of the Rambam, the Klausenberger paid a visit to the *gaon* Rabbi Asher Zev Werner. Before he left, he borrowed a volume of the Rambam's *Mishneh Torah* to learn from at the tomb. Opening the *sefer* at the tomb, the Klausenberger began reciting aloud the second chapter of *Hilchos Teshuvah*, which says that a sinner must admit his sins, and it is better to do so publically if he can.

In a broken voice, the Klausenberger said, "From the words of the Rambam it seems that it is not enough for me to repent in my own thoughts, nor is it enough for me to whisper my *teshuvah*. Rather, everyone must know what kind of person I am!" He broke down in tears and continued, "Where am I going! Even if I spend the entire day in Teveriah I will not have enough time to list all the sins that I have committed in my lifetime."

The Grave of Rav Menachem Mendel of Vitebsk

The emotional high of the Rebbe's visit to Teveriah was praying at the tomb of the tzaddik Rav Menachem Mendel of Vitebsk, author of the *Pri Ha'Aretz*, in the old cemetery of Teveriah, where many students of the Baal Shem Tov are buried. It was an awesome scene, one that left an everlasting mark on those present. The Klausenberger removed his shoes, prostrated himself on the tombstone of Reb Menachem Mendel, and cried unceasingly, as if he was purging himself of all the pain and suffering he had endured for so many years.

Later the Rebbe explained, "Ordinarily, when I visit the graves of tzaddikim of old my heart pounds, and I ask myself, 'What right do I have to come here and ask for my heart's desires?' Not so when I come to the grave of a student of the Baal Shem Tov, whose entire purpose in this world was for our generation, the one preceding the coming of Mashiach. Without them we would have no hope at all. This is especially true of Rav Menachem Mendel of Vitebsk, who was the first to establish a chassidic community in Teveriah. Here, we have a right to pray and cry out before the King."

A Letter Home

After visiting the graves of the tzaddikim, the Rebbe returned to the home of his host, Rabbi Meir Halberstam, from where he sent a short letter to his family. Writing only to his son Tzvi Elimelech, who was two years old at the time, he expressed his innermost feelings:

> *B"H, Teveriah, 5715*
> *To my dear son Tzvi Elimelech, may you live and be well,*
>
> *I heard that you desire to travel to the Holy Land. You should know that there really is something to desire. To appreciate Eretz Yisrael is not an easy matter. Only when one is as free of sins as you are can one appreciate the holiness of the land.*
>
> *May HaKadosh Baruch Hu bless you to always see the good of Yerushalayim.*

A Shabbos in Be'er Sheva

On Thursday, 21 Kislev, the Klausenberger set off for Be'er Sheva, the capital of the Negev, for the Shabbos of *Parashas Vayeishev*. His *talmidim* and followers who lived there had implored him to come and cast his influence over the residents of the city, among them many new immigrants from Romania and Hungary. The Rebbe's students arranged for him to stay in the home of Reb Yaakov Hammerman. People from all over the city came to greet the Rebbe, to receive his blessing and seek his advice. Primary among them were the local rabbis, headed by the *av beis din* Rabbi Shlomo Tena and Rabbi Eliezer Klein, *rav* of Kehillas Yere'im, who came to ask the Rebbe for his assistance in establishing a *talmud Torah* for the local children.

Many chassidim who lived in the surrounding areas and even those from afar came to Be'er Sheva to spend Shabbos with the Rebbe. "I was among those who came for that Shabbos," recalled Reb Pesach Langsam of Bnei Brak. "Standing at the doorway of the Rebbe's room, I could see that he was alone, so I quietly entered his room. He sat there learning, not sensing my entry. I stood and watched as he learned through the concluding pages of *Maseches Shabbos*. When he was done, he lifted his eyes and saw me. He stretched out his hand to take mine, and I burst into tears.

"Concerned, the Rebbe asked, 'What happened?' I told him my trouble – my first wife and all of our children had been murdered in the Holocaust. It was now already several years since I had remarried, and I had not yet been blessed with children. The doctors said that there was no chance that we would have children.

"The Rebbe immediately rebuked me, 'What's wrong with you, Pesach? The doctors say? Do we live by their word? The Creator has no say in the matter?!'

"Rising from his chair, he paced back and forth, deep in thought. Suddenly he stopped pacing and turned to me, saying with deep emotion, 'Rest assured and be confident that the salvation will soon come.'

"And so it was. A year later our first son was born."

The Shabbos in Be'er Sheva was a joyous one. The elders of the community, who remembered the courts of the Rebbe's predecessors in Europe, followed the Rebbe's every moment with teary eyes, recalling images of earlier chassidic rebbes. Those who had visited Sighet and had seen the Rebbe's first father-in-law, the Atzei Chaim, or had experienced a Shabbos in Raczfert in the court of Reb Shalom Eliezer, the Rebbe's great-uncle, now relived these experiences in the presence of the Klausenberger.

Chanukah in Petach Tikvah

On Sunday, 24 Kislev, the Rebbe traveled to Petach Tikvah to spend the week of Chanukah there. Reb Yosef Greenwald, a student of the Rebbe's father-in-law, hosted the Klausenberger in his apartment for the entire holiday.

Years later a young man from Petach Tikvah described that Shabbos Chanukah in the following way: "For the first time in my life I stood face to face with such awesome spiritual qualities... Every bone in my body trembled when I touched the Rebbe's hand and he wished me 'Good Shabbos.' I trembled even more when he asked my name and blessed me with a *yasher koach* for reciting

Birkas Kohanim, since I was among the *kohanim* there."

That week of Chanukah is remembered among Sanz chassidim as a period of great spiritual elevation. Every evening chassidim came from all over the country to watch Klausenberger lighting his Chanukah candles, singing songs of *deveikus,* and giving over *divrei Torah.* On Shabbos, the *tefillos* and *tisch*es, which were held in the large Moshav Zekeinim Synagogue on Montefiore Street, were attended by a very large congregation from Petach Tikvah and the surrounding areas.

At *shalosh seudos*, the Rebbe delivered sharp words of *mussar* about the breaches in religious observance he had seen, decrying those who were not careful to preserve Yiddish as their primary language and were educating their children in modern Hebrew. "Those who have stopped speaking Yiddish, the language of our ancestors, do not know how much damage they are causing to the environment of the Torah home," he said.

Earlier, while in Yerushalayim, the Rebbe had been honored as the *sandek* at a bris in the *beis midrash* of Congregation Kehal Emunim and spoke in defense of the holy Jewish people, even the irreligious. Several of his statements had not pleased the more zealous in Jerusalem. Now, in Petach Tikvah, one of the great *talmidei chachamim* of Yerushalayim, a grandson of Rabbi Akiva Yosef Shlesinger, *zt"l,* was seated next to the Rebbe, and the Rebbe sensed that this *talmid chacham* was aggrieved by his words.

The Rebbe turned to him and said, "If it were my intention to please the public, I would have spoken out against the use of Hebrew in Yerushalayim and would have defended the sinners and spoken against the public demonstrations about *chillul*

Shabbos in the modern city of Petach Tikvah. These remarks would undoubtedly have been much more pleasing to my listeners. But what can I do — it is my responsibility to speak about the subject that each audience needs to hear. *Chazal* teach us (*Kesubos* 105b) that if a *rav* is beloved by the residents of his city it is not because they respect him, but rather because he does not give them *mussar*."

The Source of His Vitality

Rabbi Shlomo Miller, an experienced *mohel* from Petach Tikvah, related, "After observing the Rebbe's superhuman *tefillos* and *tisches* that Shabbos, I asked my father-in-law, Rav Moshe Illevitsky, a great *talmid chacham* and contemporary of the Chazon Ish, 'How does the Rebbe have such strength? From where does he draw the strength for such *avodah* over the course of Shabbos with so little sleep or rest?'

"My father-in-law responded, 'In our town in Europe, there were merchants who during fair times could go without sleep for several days — they were so busy with their business that they didn't even feel tired. Why? They knew that the fair would provide their income for an entire year, and they didn't want to waste a minute. So it is with the Klausenberger with regard to his learning and his *tefillos*, and the rest of his *avodah* on Shabbos. He draws his vitality from this fountain, and he doesn't need any physical rest or nourishment at all.' "

The Eighth Day of Chanukah

On Sunday, the seventh day of Chanukah, the Klausenberger

left Petach Tikvah for Yerushalayim, where he lit Chanukah candles in the Chayei Olam Yeshivah in the presence of thousands of chassidim who had gathered in his honor. The following morning, after davening *shacharis* and *mussaf* in the Chassidim *beis midrash* in Batei Varshah in a service that lasted until almost noon, he conducted a *tisch* which was attended by many of the city's great *talmidei chachamim* in the home of Rabbi Yehoshua Veitzenblum.

The climax of the day came in the evening, when the Rebbe spoke at the Meah Shearim Yeshivah. Although it was a very rainy day, thousands of the Rebbe's followers braved the rain and cold to hear him. As was his custom, he began with a very complex discussion of the laws of Chanukah, then continued with words of *mussar* and *hashkafah* connected to the *chag*, calling on his audience to increase their love and unity among themselves, both in order to strengthen each individual and to strengthen the community against the negative influences of the outside.

"The miracle of Chanukah came about," the Rebbe declared, "because of the unity of spirit among the *tehorim*, the tzaddikim, and the *oskei Torah*, unlike a regular war, in which by nature every commander has his own idea and approach to fighting."

The Rebbe also spoke with great concern about the grave danger posed by Reform Judaism and other such movements that were attempting to redefine and modernize Judaism. He noted that in the Grace after Meals we first thank the Creator for having given us Eretz Yisrael, and only afterwards do we thank Him for having taken us out of Egypt. "Shouldn't we keep things in their historical sequence and first thank Hashem for having taken us out of Egypt, and then only afterwards for having given us the land?" he asked.

"From this we can learn," he explained, "that even after we have settled in Eretz Yisrael we are still vulnerable to the influence of Mitzrayim. Even in Eretz Yisrael it is possible to sin with the abominations of Egypt, and one must be on guard against this. We therefore thank Hashem not only for having given us this beloved land but also for protecting us here from negative influences."

After the Klausenberger's speech, the large audience went to the nearby Bais Yaakov building on Rechov Admon for a *chanukas habayis* attended by all the great rabbinic leaders of Yerushalayim. The Rebbe, who, as mentioned above, was a great supporter of the school, gave an impassioned address on the obligation to strengthen girls' education to the same degree as boys' education.

Last Days in Eretz Yisrael

The Klausenberger remained in Eretz Yisrael for another week after Chanukah, in which he continued visiting various communities and serving as Rebbe to all who needed him.

On Tuesday, the third of Teves, the Rebbe visited Moshav Mishmar HaShivah, where he dedicated a new building that had been purchased for a She'eris HaPleitah elementary school and gave instructions to the local community leaders regarding the operation of the school.

On Thursday, the fifth of Teves, the Rebbe visited Tel Aviv and conducted a *tisch* in honor of the *yahrtzeit* of his great-uncle, the Divrei Yechezkel of Shinov. Many chassidim attended this *tisch*, including a number of elderly chassidim who had known the Divrei Yechezkel personally.

After the *tisch*, the Klausenberger went to the nearby home of the Belzer Rebbe for a farewell blessing before his return to America. The Belzer Rebbe greeted the Klausenberger with great joy, just as he had seven weeks earlier. As the Klausenberger recounted his experiences in Eretz Yisrael, the Belzer Rebbe said to him, "Klausenberger Rav, I am jealous of you. I do not have that same level of 'And Moshe came down from the mountain to the people' as you do. Perhaps this is a spark from the soul of Shmuel HaNavi, who traveled all over Eretz Yisrael to stir the hearts of the people to *avodas Hashem!*"

As they parted, the Belzer Rebbe escorted the Klausenberger to the door and, placing one hand on the mezuzah and stretching the other to the Klausenberger, blessed him, "May the Almighty watch over you so that no harm shall come your way and so that no one will be able to hurt you or me." Then he repeated, "Not me and not you."

After the Rebbe left, the Belzer Rebbe turned to his assistant, Reb Shalom Fogel, and said, "Did you see his holy presence? This is a Jew who has achieved great *yiras Shamayim.*"

"It Is Difficult to Leave Eretz Yisrael"

The Klausenberger spent his final Shabbos in Eretz Yisrael, Shabbos *Parashas Vayigash*, in the city of Bnei Brak. A festive atmosphere filled the city as hundreds came to greet the Rebbe at the home of his host, Reb Yechiel Benedict, a well-known figure who hosted many great Torah scholars in his home. Thousands came to daven with the Rebbe and attend his *tisch*es, which were held in the Chug Chasam Sofer Beis Midrash. It was a memorable Shabbos that was not quickly forgotten.

The Rebbe stayed in Bnei Brak for one more day and then traveled to Lod Airport on Monday morning, the ninth of Teves. A long motorcade of cars and buses filled with chassidim accompanied him to the airport. Many others came from all over the country to bid him farewell.

It was very difficult for the Klausenberger to leave the Holy Land. Before boarding the aircraft, he turned to say good-bye to his followers, his voice choked with emotion. Tears streamed down his face as he spoke of the blessings of the Holy Land and repeated the words of Dovid HaMelech, "For Your servants hold her stones dear and cherish her very dust" (*Tehillim* 102:15).

"When I arrived," he related, "I wanted to fulfill the literal meaning of this verse, but I remembered the words of the Gemara, 'Rabbi Abba would kiss the stones of Akko' (*Kesubos* 112a), and I thought, why specifically Akko? Tosafos explain that this is based on a passage in the *Yerushalmi*, which states that half the city was in Eretz Yisrael and half of it was in *chutz la'aretz*. Only when Rabbi Abba was standing specifically in this divided city was he able to discern the difference between the holiness of Eretz Yisrael and the impurity of *chutz la'aretz*.

"The difference was so obvious then that Rabbi Abba was moved to literally kiss the stones in the section of Akko that was in Eretz Yisrael. So too with me. Only after one steps foot in the Holy Land can one see the ray of light that emanates from this good land; a land which great men loved, this awesome and beautiful mountain."

The Rebbe encouraged his followers to walk proudly in the paths of our forefathers and to attach themselves to the chassidic way of life. He did not say anything publicly about the investigations he had conducted, while traveling the length and breadth of the land, for a site that would allow him to fulfill his dreams of settling in Eretz Yisrael. In the recesses of his heart, though, he felt that the day would soon come when he would settle in Eretz Yisrael and build a beautiful city of Torah, with chassidim faithfully following the teachings of the Baal Shem Tov and serving as a stellar example for all.

When the Klausenberger boarded the plane, he viewed himself as a Jew from Eretz Yisrael who was leaving only temporarily, for the sake of a mitzvah — just like the tzaddik Rav Menachem Mendel of Vitebsk, who left Teveriah many years before to strengthen the Jews of Europe and encourage them to move to Eretz Yisrael.

Chapter 9

Actualizing the Dream of Kiryat Sanz

A Community in Eretz Yisrael

Part of the Rebbe's goal in his first visit to Eretz Yisrael was to find an appropriate site for the future city of Kiryat Sanz. Just as Hashem had commanded Avraham, "Live in the land that I shall command you," the Klausenberger Rebbe heard a Divine command instructing him, "Build a city in My land."

The Rebbe's heart's desire was to rebuild what had been destroyed. He wanted to bring Jews from all over the diaspora to settle in Eretz Yisrael, and especially to renew the chassidic lifestyle of Sanz of old in this new city. He wanted an exact replica of Sanz of Galicia, a place that would be a vibrant Torah center in which *limud haTorah*, *avodas Hashem*, and *gemillus chassadim* would flourish.

Searching for a Site

In his search for a suitable location, the Rebbe spoke with

many of the leaders of the Torah world about his dream. Some suggested that he build the city on the outskirts of Tzefas, while others suggested Be'er Sheva in the Negev. The Gerrer Rebbe, the Lev Simchah, suggested several locations in the Sharon, in the center of the country. For various reasons, none of these locations worked out.

The Rebbe was also approached with the idea of establishing his new community in Yerushalayim, but he declined, explaining, "*Baruch Hashem*, Yerushalayim has a special holiness and much Torah learning. I want to add a new city to the landscape of Eretz Yisrael which will increase the light of Torah in our holy land." For this reason, the Rebbe also rejected Bnei Brak as a site for the new Kiryat Sanz.

When the Rebbe returned to America, he asked several of his followers to continue the search for a suitable location. He created an action committee for this purpose and appointed Reb Mendel Frankel, Reb Yechezkel Neuwirth, Reb Chaim Alter Roth, Reb Yehoshua Veitzenblum, and Reb David Greenzweig as the committee members.

These five committee members spent the following summer investigating several possible locations for the new Kiryat Sanz and eventually brought the Rebbe their results. They had found two possible locations suitable for the Rebbe's purposes: one slightly west of the Mediterranean, between Netanyah and a village called Kfar Yonah, and the other in Netanyah itself, in an area called Pardes HaGedud. They asked the Rebbe which he preferred.

An Island of Holiness

After some deliberation, the Rebbe called the committee on *erev Rosh HaShanah* 1955 to tell them that he preferred Pardes HaGedud over the other site. Although Netanyah was a predominately secular city, the Rebbe had no hesitations — quite the contrary, he hoped to create an island of holiness in this sea of secularity that would bring light to the entire city.

When those close to him reminded him of the challenges awaiting him in Netanyah because of its distance from other large religious communities, the Rebbe responded in surprise. "I am horrified, absolutely horrified! I always knew that goyim do not properly appreciate the strength of the Jewish people, and that non-*frum* Jews do not properly appreciate the strength of *frum* Jews. But it is a great mystery to me why we have skeptics even amongst ourselves — people who do not recognize what we are capable of accomplishing ourselves, *b'siyatta diShmaya.*"

Buying Land

The Rebbe instructed the committee members to buy the tracts of land under discussion in his name, giving them power of attorney to do so, immediately after Rosh HaShanah.

Later, recalling the purchase of the area of Kiryat Sanz, the Rebbe cited the words of Rabbeinu Bachya, who noted that the majority of Eretz Yisrael was acquired by the nations through battle, but the three holiest places were purchased: Me'aras HaMachpeilah in Chevron was purchased by Avraham, Har HaMoriah was purchased by David HaMelech, and Har Gerizim and Har Eival, where *b'nei*

Yisrael accepted the Torah, were purchased by Yaakov. "From this we learn," the Rebbe explained, "that any land destined for a holy purpose in the history of the Jewish people must be purchased for value, and under no circumstances may it be received for free." In addition, he added, "*Chazal* have spoken at length on the value of every mitzvah, particularly when one pays full price for it."

On the third day of Tishrei 1954, the committee members met with the owners of the land in order to finalize the purchase deals and give a deposit. [In later years, the Israel Land Authority gave the community additional land, which was added to the areas purchased privately by the Rebbe.]

"Kiryat Sanz"

The news of the purchase was received in the Rebbe's Williamsburg home with immense joy and rejoicing. Toasting "*l'chaim*" at the end of Tzom Gedalyah, the Rebbe envisioned the dawn of a new era in Eretz Yisrael. The chassidim present that evening spent a few minutes discussing potential names for the new community that the Rebbe was developing. The Rebbe surprised them all by suddenly opening his desk drawer and removing a small note, on which the words *Kiryat Sanz* had been written in large letters.

Six months later, on 21 Adar, 1956, the Rebbe realized his dream when he went to Eretz Yisrael to lay the cornerstone for Kiryat Sanz.

(The Rebbe originally planned to have the cornerstone-laying ceremony on Tu B'Av, since *Chazal* say in *Maseches Taanis* that "there were no days in Israel as good as Tu B'Av and Purim" [*Taanis* 26b]. However, the Belzer Rebbe pointed out to him that perhaps it was not appropriate to make a celebration on this day, since it was his father's *yahrtzeit*. The Rebbe therefore pushed the celebration up to the twenty-first of Adar.)

Preparing for the Cornerstone Laying

On the seventeenth of Adar, the day after Shushan Purim, the Rebbe left for Israel. A day later he landed at Lod Airport, where the hundreds of chassidim were waiting to greet him. They broke out in song, overjoyed at the awesomeness of the event. The Rebbe had come to lay the cornerstone for Kiryat Sanz! The Rebbe would be moving to the Holy Land!

Directly from the airport, the Rebbe traveled to Netanyah, where he stayed at the home of his relative Shlomo Stern, a descendant of Dinov and Ropshitz. The next day, after a brief trip to Pardes HaGedud to see the site that had been purchased for Kiryat Sanz, the Rebbe went to Tel Aviv to visit the Belzer Rebbe. Then he returned to Netanyah and began preparing for Shabbos.

Chassidim from all over Eretz Yisrael came to Netanyah to spend Shabbos with the Rebbe. The city was transformed overnight. The local residents could hardly believe their eyes: For the first time, the streets of the city were filled with chassidim in their traditional garb; men with beards and *pei'os* and beards, wearing tzitzis, *shtreimels*, and long coats. The davening and *tisches*, held in the large local shul, were spiritually elevating for one and all.

An Emotional Prayer

On Sunday, the twenty-first of Adar, the *yahrtzeit* of Rabbi Elimelech of Lizhensk, the Noam Elimelech, the Rebbe prepared for the cornerstone-laying ceremony. Rabbi Eliyahu Shmuel Schmerler, the Klausenberg *rosh yeshivah*, recalled, "Even before sunrise the Rebbe was dressed in his *shtreimel* and Shabbos *kapota*. *Shacharis* took a very long time, several hours, as the Rebbe prayed with great intensity and with undescribable concentration. I can still hear the sweet sound of his words as he recited, '*Ezras avoseinu atah hu mei'olam* — The helper of our forefathers are You alone, forever, Shield and Savior for their children after them in every generation...' Again and again the Rebbe repeated these words, his voice rising in a special melody. I shall never forget how he recited, '*Lariv rivam la'avos u'lebanim* — to take up their grievance for fathers and for sons.' The sound of his cries reverberates in my mind to this very day."

Thousands of *frum* Jews gathered in Netanyah for this momentous day, many of whom had connections to Sanz Chassidus and others of whom were Holocaust survivors who knew the Rebbe from Germany. Rabbi Yisrael Ehrlich opened the ceremony on behalf of the She'eiris Haplietah Committee. He was followed by Rabbi Avraham Werner, Rabbi of Netanyah, who expressed his hope and dream that the new settlement of Torah and Chassidus would inspire the entire area and become a great and influential religious center. Other speakers, leaders of religious Jewry, noted that the start of construction of Kiryat Sanz was a great and momentous day in the history of world Jewry.

"On Mount Zion There Shall Be a Refuge"

The main address was delivered by the Klausenberger. Beaming with joy, the Rebbe began by relating that on the eve of his embarkment for Eretz Yisrael, many people in America had asked him why he was traveling to Israel at a time when the political situation in the country was so volatile. "Does it make sense to invest so much work and capital in a place surrounded by enemies and murderers?" they asked.

In answer, the Rebbe pointed out that Divine providence had arranged for the laying of the cornerstone of Kiryat Sanz on the 170th *yahrtzeit* of the Noam Elimelech. According to tradition, this great tzaddik had said that he had nullified the suffering of the Jewish people prior to the coming of Mashiach. When Hitler, *yemach shemo,* came to power, many Jews were baffled. What had happened to the promise of the Noam Elimelech?

"It would seem to me," the Rebbe thundered, "that the promise of Rebbe Elimelech referred to the portion of *klal Yisrael* here in Eretz Yisrael.

"There is an eternal divine promise that Hashem will never forsake us," the Rebbe continued. "Even in the valley of death of Auschwitz, I said to the *Yidden* near me, 'Do not fear. The Master of the Universe Himself is with us here even in the gas chambers.' To that non-Jewish doctor who asked me, 'What will become of the Jewish people?' I answered confidently, 'In the end Hitler will be destroyed, and *klal Yisrael* will live forever.' 'How do you know this?' he asked. I answered, 'Over the past two thousand years, many people have tried to destroy us, but Hashem has saved us from their hands. Even when the most brutal enemy rises against us, there will always be a surviving remnant. And it seems to me now that Eretz Yisrael is the place designated for the fulfillment of this promise.

"Even in the days of the *churban habayis*, we davened for the rebuilding of Yerushalayim. Throughout the years of *galus*, our eyes have always been focused on this land. When the evil Titus planned to destroy us and decreed the death of every Jew, *chas v'chalilah*, he certainly never imagined that 1,880 years later Jewish people would be laying the cornerstone for Kiryat Sanz in our Holy Land!"

Our Only Haven

The Rebbe also added that he was sure that had Hitler decreed death only upon the Jews he would have been killed immediately, since misfortune that only affects *klal Yisrael* is always nullified. All the suffering and destruction came upon us only because Hitler declared war on all the nations of the world at once.

"Today," he continued, "the entire world fears the atom bomb. Here, in Eretz Yisrael, we fear the nations of Yishmael surrounding us. Outside of Eretz Yisrael we have a common danger, a danger shared by Jews and non-Jews alike, and it is therefore a real threat. But here in Eretz Yisrael, where the danger affects only *klal Yisrael*, these dangers will undoubtedly be nullified. This situation will not endure! We will be protected under the shade of the Shechinah. Therefore, I say to all who ask about my presence here today, 'I am escaping to Eretz Yisrael in order to save my life and the lives of many other Jews — for this is our only haven.' "

Drawing Strength from Previous Generations

The Rebbe continued his speech by speaking at great length about the holiness of Eretz Yisrael. He stressed the fact that all the wonders and merits of the land only exist when *klal Yisrael* observe the Torah and perform the mitzvos, whereas one who sins in Eretz Yisrael commits a much worse offense than one who sins outside the land.

Indeed, the first ones to resettle in Eretz Yisrael, some two hundred years before, the Rebbe pointed out, were pure and Torah-true Jews, disciples of the Baal Shem Tov, who came to Eretz Yisrael with great *mesiras nefesh*. The great Rabbis Hillel of Kalamy and Akiva Yosef Shlesinger founded Petach Tikvah and other such communities.

The Rebbe related how several days before, he had been given a letter written by his great-uncle, Rabbi Shalom Eliezer of Raczfert, shortly before the Holocaust, to one of his followers in Eretz Yisrael. Pleading for a visa to enter Palestine, Reb Shalom Eliezer mentioned that his father, the Divrei Chaim, "had a tremendous desire to travel to Eretz Yisrael" but was unable to do so.

"Let us draw strength from the longing of this tzaddik, and from the longing of all the tzaddikim who wished to move to Eretz Yisrael, and hope to Hashem that He will allow us to be successful in building a town that will be faithful to Hashem and His Torah," the Rebbe concluded.

The Time Is Now

The climax of the Rebbe's speech was his call to Torah-observant Jews everywhere to settle in the Land of Israel.

"It is my opinion," he declared, "that at a time like this, when every Jew has the opportunity to move to Eretz Yisrael, and there are already many *frum* Jews living here, and despite all the difficulties everyone can serve Hashem as he wishes to, every Jew, wherever he may be, has an obligation to settle in Eretz Yisrael. In this way we can prepare ourselves properly for the coming of Mashiach!"

This historic call to action reverberated throughout the world and made an immense impact on Jews throughout the Diaspora.

A Plan for the Future

At the conclusion of his address, the Rebbe briefly described his plan for the new city. "Hundreds of families will move to Kiryat Sanz from *chutz la'aretz* and establish roots here, living their lives according to our holy Torah and our *mesorah*. In the center of the city, there will be a yeshivah and educational institutions for both boys and girls, to educate them in Torah and *yiras Shamayim*. We will build businesses and factories that will provide the families who move here with an honorable livelihood and steady income.

"Today is a day of great celebration for me," he continued. "I have often thought to myself, 'Why did I remain among the living? Why did I alone survive from my entire family?' Today, I know clearly that everything happened so that I should merit to lay, with my very own hands, the cornerstone of Kiryat Sanz in Eretz Yisrael."

An Old and Foolish King

When the Klausenberger went to lay the cornerstone of Kiryat Sanz, he said, "I have always wondered why the *yetzer hara* is referred to as '*melech zakein u'ksil*' – an old and foolish king. Why should he be called foolish, when he is known for his craftiness, seducing man to sin with ingenious tactics and devices?

"I have observed, however, that he is indeed a fool. It is just that at times his foolishness only becomes clear when he is old. Our city of Netanyah is a clear example of this. At the time of its founding, the *yetzer hara* advised its founders to include a special provision in its charter prohibiting the building of a synagogue. Yet today, thirty years later, even in the modern city of Netanyah there are shuls and a community of *frum* Jews. Thus, in the end, we see that the *yetzer hara* was a fool when he thought that he could ensure that at least one city in Eretz Yisrael would not have a shul.

"This is true about all of the *yetzer hara*'s plans, which are intended to bring destruction upon *klal Yisrael*, or make them forget the Torah, *chas v'chalilah*! He also wants to force us to publicly renounce our portion in the G-d of Israel, just like the Greeks did in their time."

Heaven on Earth

Shortly after the cornerstone-laying ceremony, a Jewish American journalist named Nissan Gordon asked the Rebbe if it was correct that the Rebbe had said that in these turbulent times, the safest place in the world for a Jew is in the Land of Israel.

In answer, the Rebbe opened a *Midrash Rabbah*, opened it to *Parashas Va'eschanan*, and read aloud the following passage:

> *Every misfortune that comes to the Jewish nation and the nations of the world together is a misfortune, while misfortune that comes only to the Jews is not a misfortune. Rabbi Yochanan explained, for example the misfortune in Shushan, which affected only the Jews, as it says, "A great mourning for the Jews" (Esther 4:3). Immediately Hashem sprouted the seeds of salvation. How do we know? Because the verse states, "For the Jews there was light and joy" (ibid. 8:16).*

"In Eretz Yisrael," the Rebbe explained, "where Jews suffer from an enemy which only affects the Jewish people, there is nothing to fear, for this type of misfortune will vanish speedily. This is not true anywhere else in the world, where Jews and non-Jews live together in constant fear of what will happen tomorrow, fearing the atom bomb and nuclear missiles."

"If this is so," the reporter pressed, "what is the Rebbe going to say upon his return to the Jews of America?"

"I am planning to tell them that if they want to be sure that their children will remain Jews they should quickly pack their bags and move to Eretz Yisrael. There is no land in the world as wondrous as this one."

"But they hear negative reports about the level of *Yiddishkeit* here," the reporter pressed.

The Rebbe smiled and responded with a hint of sarcasm, "Just because Adam and Chavah sinned in Gan Eden, did that mean that it was no longer Gan Eden?"

Chapter 10

Aliyah at Last

Longings for the Holy Land

The Rebbe's longing for the land of Eretz Yisrael was so deep it is impossible to capture it in words. Each day that he remained in the Diaspora was painful, as is evident in his writing during that period in his life. On *erev Pesach*, 1958, he wrote to the Sanzer chassidim in Yerushalayim imploring them to pray for "my miserable soul which sits in a dark and desolate land, far from our life's source."

The following year, between Pesach and Shavous, the Klausenberger traveled to Eretz Yisrael for a very short visit to deal with a number of matters concerning the development of Kiryat Sanz. For various reasons, the Rebbe had to return to the United States quickly, and during a layover in Zurich he wrote a letter to followers in Yerushalayim which offers a glimpse into his heart:

"I am so sad and my heart is broken that just before the holiday of Shavous, at the very time when *klal Yisrael* would ascend to Yerushalayim in a spirit of gratitude to spend the holiday there, I am leaving the source of the existence of the soul... I very much envy you who have been blessed to live in land of the Almighty. If only I had the wings of a dove, I would fly to the desert and live in the stone crevices of the mountains of Yehudah and Yerushalayim!"

The Rebbe concluded by thanking the Almighty that he merited "to be in the Holy Land for the past several days, even though I did not do anything there. Due to our many sins I was preoccupied with worries and concerns and did not feel any of the awesome light of holiness of the Land...but for a lowly and shameful person like myself, just walking in the Holy Land and breathing its air which makes one wise was an amazing kindness from the Almighty... Just as He has begun to shower His kindness and goodness upon me, so shall He enable me to live permanently in Eretz Yisrael."

The Decision Is Made

With the approach of Kislev of 1959, the thirteenth anniversary of the Rebbe's immigration to America, the Rebbe decided that the time had come to move permanently to Eretz Yisrael. Years later the Rebbe would joke that he did not want to celebrate his "bar mitzvah" in America.

In a letter to his trusted follower Reb Yehudah Belz, the Rebbe requested that the yeshivah students and chassidim recite *Tehillim* and pray for him, "that our trip should be safe and blessed...and without any difficulties or mishaps, and that we should merit to come to Eretz Yisrael and settle there with our entire family and all who are accompanying us."

The Rebbe further requested that special emissaries be sent to Tzefas, Meron, and Teveriah to pray at the graves of his ancestor the Toltsheva Rebbe, the holy Rabbi Mendele of Vitebsk, and the other tzaddikim buried in this area. In the merit of these holy rabbis, he wrote, Hashem would have mercy "on us and our family and we shall merit to ascend to Zion in happiness and see the lights of our Holy Land together with all of Israel."

The Rebbe also requested that his followers not announce his coming with extensive publicity, for the greatest honor to Hashem results from doing things with privacy and modesty. "If it were possible to come in complete secrecy," he wrote, "it would be much better, but in any case, not in the way of the hasty ones who try to demonstrate their greatness with large advertisements."

This last request, however, was not to be fulfilled, for as soon as the Klausenberger's decision to move to Eretz Yisrael became public, tens of his chassidim and their families, gripped by the idea of moving to the Holy Land, sold their businesses, packed their belongings, and made plans to settle in Eretz Yisrael, too. News of this large aliyah, reminiscent of historic aliyot like that of the students of the Baal Shem Tov in the late eighteenth century, made waves throughout the Jewish world.

A Historic Journey

After months of careful preparation, the date of the Rebbe's move to Eretz Yisrael was set for Sunday, 19 Kislev, 1959. The émigrés were accompanied to Idlewild Airport in New York with much song and dance. After an emotional farewell, the Rebbe and his followers boarded a specially chartered aircraft for the journey to their new home.

Despite the Rebbe's requests that everything should be done quietly, without any publicity, his followers in Eretz Yisrael could not restrain themselves and throngs streamed to the airport to welcome him.

As the wheels of the large plane touched down on the runway at Lod Airport, thousands of hearts were beating with unparalleled intensity, joy, and anticipation. The doors swung open, the stairs were rolled out, and the Klausenberger's silhouette appeared in the doorway of the plane.

The Rebbe descended the stairs accompanied by his young children and his devoted chassid, Reb Menashe Klein, who was carrying a *sefer Torah*. They were followed down the stairs by chassidim of all ages, parents and children holding hands as they took their first steps on the soil of Eretz Yisrael. Reb Yudel Turner, a devoted chassid of the Rebbe, held a violin in his hand.

Cries of "*Baruch haba!*" filled the air. Chassidim waiting in the airport broke out in dance, singing over and over again, "*Or zarua latzaddik.*"

"Baruch Hashem"

The Klausenberger faced the crowd, which included delegations of government and community leaders who came to welcome him. Acknowledging one and all, the Rebbe said, "*Baruch Hashem.* I am happy and indebted to the Ribbono Shel Olam that we have merited to see this day."

A man in the crowd, not a chassid of the Rebbe, called out boldly, "Why have you moved here?"

The Rebbe answered briefly, "From the day the Beis HaMikdash was destroyed Jews have been returning to the Holy

Land — and I am one of them." Then he added, "I am moving to Eretz Yisrael not for my own honor and not for the honor of my ancestors but to do the will of our Father in Heaven and to serve Him with all my heart!"

He expressed a hope that many other Jews in the Diaspora would do as he had done and move to Eretz Yisrael. The Rebbe predicted that the town he was developing in Netanyah would soon become a metropolis of Torah and *Yiddishkeit* that would serve as a model for every city in the Jewish world.

"Today," he announced confidently, "people call Kiryat Sanz a town near Netanyah. In the future, they will say that Netanyah is a town near Kiryat Sanz."

A Day of Celebration

In the years that followed, the Rebbe celebrated the nineteenth of Kislev, the day on which he left America for Eretz Yisrael, as a holiday. The following year he related, "I was unsure whether I should celebrate the day on which I left America or the following day, on which I arrived in Eretz Yisrael. I decided to celebrate on the nineteenth of Kislev because the primary joy was leaving America. Just like Rabbi Shneur Zalman of Liadi celebrated his release from prison on this day, so I celebrate the day that I left America and was saved from its depraved society.

"Even today," he continued with great excitement, "after living here a full year I do not fully comprehend the greatness of Eretz Yisrael, for to do so one must be at a very high spiritual level. But we can learn from our holy forefathers who spent their whole lives longing for Eretz Yisrael.

"Even in earlier generations, when the journey to Eretz Yisrael was fraught with danger, the great Rabbi Ovadyah of Bartenura risked his life and traveled for three years to reach the Holy Land. Before him the Ramban, Rabbi Yehudah HaLevi, and many other holy scholars made the difficult journey to the Holy Land. These holy men truly sensed the sanctity of Eretz Yisrael. Nothing was more valuable to them. How can we answer to them?"

Without Calculations

A short time later, the Klausenberger wrote to a *talmid* in America who asked if he should make aliyah, "The Torah tells us to 'come and inherit the land.' We only need to come and as a result we shall inherit. Just as *klal Yisrael* accepted the Torah without qualification or calculation simply by declaring, '*Naaseh v'nishma*,' moving to Eretz Yisrael should be done without calculations."

(The Rebbe would often comment that when Yehoshua ben Nun conquered Eretz Yisrael, he vanquished the King of Cheshbon — a play on words, since the word *cheshbon* means "calculations.")

"Hurry as quickly as you can to move to the Holy Land, the sooner the better," he continued. "Do not say, 'I will come later'; instead, be like Nachshon ben Aminadav [who jumped into the sea without hesitations]. I bless you that you merit to move to our Holy Land immediately and be blessed with the blessing of Hashem from Zion."

The Dawn of a New Era

The day of the Rebbe's immigration to Eretz Yisrael was cause for rejoicing for all of Torah Jewry. For the Klausenberger's aliyah was not the aliyah of a single person or family, or even of a group of people. Rather, it was the aliyah of an entire movement, which included communities from all over the world. It was an aliyah which signified a new era, both in Eretz Yisrael and in the Diaspora, since many others quickly followed in his footsteps.

It was a new beginning.

The Sanz-Klausenberg Dynasty

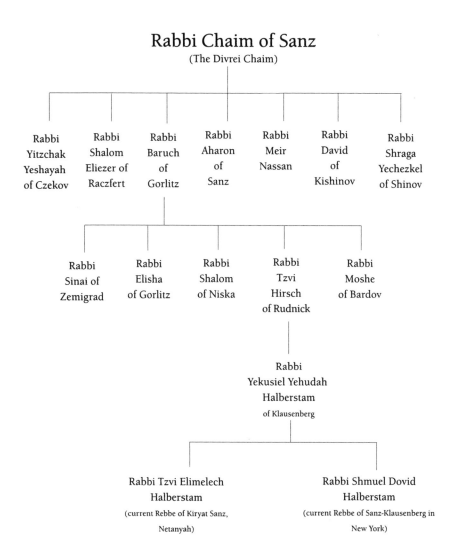

Rabbi Chaim of Sanz
(The Divrei Chaim)

| Rabbi Yitzchak Yeshayah of Czekov | Rabbi Shalom Eliezer of Raczfert | Rabbi Baruch of Gorlitz | Rabbi Aharon of Sanz | Rabbi Meir Nassan | Rabbi David of Kishinov | Rabbi Shraga Yechezkel of Shinov |

| Rabbi Sinai of Zemigrad | Rabbi Elisha of Gorlitz | Rabbi Shalom of Niska | Rabbi Tzvi Hirsch of Rudnick | Rabbi Moshe of Bardov |

Rabbi Yekusiel Yehudah Halberstam
of Klausenberg

| Rabbi Tzvi Elimelech Halberstam | Rabbi Shmuel Dovid Halberstam |
| (current Rebbe of Kiryat Sanz, Netanyah) | (current Rebbe of Sanz-Klausenberg in New York) |